T0267106

ENGLAND'S CALAMITY?

ENGLAND'S CALAMITY?

A New Interpretation of the
'Match of the Century'

CHRIS JONES

First published by Pitch Publishing, 2023

Pitch Publishing
9 Donnington Park,
85 Birdham Road,
Chichester,
West Sussex,
PO20 7AJ
www.pitchpublishing.co.uk
info@pitchpublishing.co.uk

© 2023, Chris Jones

Every effort has been made to trace the copyright.
Any oversight will be rectified in future editions at the
earliest opportunity by the publisher.

All rights reserved. No part of this book may be reproduced,
sold or utilised in any form or transmitted in any form or by
any means, electronic or mechanical, including photocopying,
recording or by any information storage and retrieval system,
without prior permission in writing from the Publisher.

A CIP catalogue record is available for this book
from the British Library.

ISBN 978 1 80150 415 7

Typesetting and origination by Pitch Publishing
Printed and bound in Great Britain by TJ Books Ltd, Padstow

CONTENTS

PART ONE: BEFORE

Introduction

IN HIS popular Pelican title from 1951, *The Greeks*, the classicist H.D.F. Kitto elucidates on the monumental date in ancient Greek history where the unbelievable happened – the Spartan army lost in the field of battle in a straight fight. This mind-boggling defeat took place in 371 BC at Leuctra and the foundations of Greek society were irreparably shifted. The victors were the Thebans under the leadership of Pelopidas and Epaminondas. They didn't assure victory by the simple solution of a vastly superior military force; they did it by devising a new and innovative military tactic.

Engaged military conflict in ancient Greece had, previously, followed a highly predictable pattern, with opposing forces lined up in a tight phalanx of heavy infantry eight men deep. The two lines then came together in brutal face-to-face combat. The Theban generals developed a new system where they reduced one side and the centre and packed the other wing with a depth of around 50 men. This concentrated pack of men just smashed their way through the Spartan lines and the passage of Greece's future was irrevocably changed. It wasn't hugely sophisticated, but it worked. A group of men sat down and thought through a series of issues and problems to see how they could become victorious in their specific field.

Some 2,324 years later the Hungarian national football team, the *Aranycsapat*, or Golden Squad, replicated the role of the Thebans. Their planned approach to the clash with England in November 1953 put their opponents' amateurish outlook to the sword just as clearly as the fallen Spartan soldiers. Football in England would change, at least in part, due to the national team's 6-3 defeat at Wembley. However, the long-argued point that it was an instant revolution involving all areas of the English football world is somewhat of a myth. The crux of the matter was the sometimes intense split between two opposing outlooks. On one side were those in the game who wanted to see change with a broad expansion of coaching and tactics, and then there were those who harked back to a perceived Golden Age where England reigned supreme. This divide would shape the game in England for the next decade and beyond.

Since the England players trudged off the Wembley pitch after their 6-3 destruction at the hands of Hungary on 25 November 1953 there has been endless comment and analysis of this match and how it stood as the point of change between the old and modern worlds of English football. It made its way into near endless commentary from football journalists, writers and commentators but also moving into wider fields such as Jean-Luc Godard's 2004 film *Notre musique* and the 2003 book *Budapest* by Chico Buarque, a Brazilian writer who named several characters in the novel after the Hungarian players. The popular image from 70 years removed is that managers, coaches, players, administrators and writers went sprinting down Wembley Way to the Tube station to set up wide-reaching committees and quangos, who drew up an unshakeable template for rapid change that was religiously followed by every team in the land. The reality was much more nuanced and layered. There was no immediate revolution but a much slower, sporadic evolution for which a very small number of people had already sown the seeds for.

The 6-3 defeat and its sister slaughter of 7-1 in Budapest six months later acted as a fulcrum of tensions between those who wanted to twist and those who felt it was necessary to stick. In 1953 there were limited options for a televisual experience of a game. If you wanted to experience a match and analyse it for yourself, you physically went to the ground. It didn't matter whether that was Wembley or Port Vale, Newcastle United or Halifax Town. On that late-November day a packed Wembley acted as a vast magnetic force attracting absolutely anyone and everyone of consequence in the English game, both in 1953 and for the next 25 years.

The importance of this match lies in the broad range of characters, individuals and personalities present in the world's then most famous football stadium. Important and never-ending tropes of the game were represented through the patriarch (Stanley Rous), the boffin (Walter Winterbottom), the incomparable (Stanley Matthews), the golden boy (Billy Wright) and the one-cap wonder (Ernie Taylor). They all brought their perspective to this game and the post-match commentary. Their roles and positions brought forward a myriad of semi-explanations and excuses heard by any follower of football since the 1860s: the endless stream of excuses for a football defeat.

Postcards From the Era of Perceived Superiority

A MAJOR question of all historical enquiry is where do we start in terms of space and time? Do we start at the beginning of the organised game? The 19th-century codification of several disparate games had brought clear lines of division between association and rugby football. The rise of professionalism in the clubs of the north-west of England and the employment of a new breed of players coming down from Scotland ended forever the domination of the game by the amateurs of The Wanderers and the Royal Engineers. The pattern of English club football was strongly established by the likes of Preston North End, Blackburn Rovers, Everton and Aston Villa. English professional football became innately connected to the world of factories, mills, shipyards and coal mines. A world of rigidity and patterns, where the repetition of clocks, shifts and timetables dominated. So perhaps Scotland v England in Glasgow in 1872 is a start point or Portugal v England in Lisbon in 1947 or three years later at USA v England in the Brazil World Cup of 1950?

An appropriate place to begin seems to be the founding of FIFA in 1904 and the complex relationship and non-relationship between FIFA and the Football Association from 1904 to 1947. The Fédération International de Football Association was founded in May 1904 with a small group of original members – France, Belgium, Switzerland, Sweden, Spain, Holland and Denmark. Not exactly world-encompassing; more a western European federation. The FA (Football Association), as football's Mother Country, were invited to join from the inception. The original codifier of the game had to receive an invite to this nascent body. At first Frederick Wall, secretary of the FA, concluded, probably in about seven seconds, that there was absolutely nothing to gain from joining this little, French-led grouping. The same year may well have been the year of the *Entente Cordiale* between Britain and France at governmental level, but no one at the FA seemed to be aware of a new, formal relationship. However the year after the FA did relent and no matter how reluctantly joined FIFA.

The spectacular arrogance of the rulers of the English game was confirmed four years later when England embarked on their first international tour around continental Europe. In four games they destroyed the best that *Mitteleuropa* had to offer. Austria were dispatched 6-1 and 11-1 in Vienna, Hungary 7-0 in Budapest and Bohemia 4-0 in Prague. In 1909, there was another tour of central Europe resulting in three more consecutive victories – 4-2 and 8-2 v Hungary, and 8-1 v Austria. In two consecutive summers England played seven matches on tour and scored 48 goals, with a straight run of victories. The belief that England were the paramount masters was hegemonic, and the English never gave anyone a rest from communicating the position that they alone held their omnipresence on Mount Olympus. Britain, in general, was the undisputed home of football and the original masters of the game: the codifiers and initiators who established both the international and professional aspects of football, who then through cultural imperialism exported it across Europe and Latin America. British engineers, sailors, soldiers and businessmen stashed footballs in their luggage and booted them down the gangplank to found the game across major international cities.

The explosion in the popularity of the England v Scotland and Rangers v Celtic matches only confirmed the pre-eminence of all things British in the microcosm of pre-World War One football. By 1912 Celtic Park and Ibrox were accommodating 74,000 and 65,000 for the Old Firm derbies. Scotland's national football stadium, Hampden Park, was recording colossal crowds of 100,000 in 1906, expanding to 127,000 by 1912. It was this tale of continued expansion of the game that led to Britain's clear view that football in the British Isles between 1870 and 1914 had a position unrivalled anywhere else in the world.

An important force in the expansion of the game was mass media, which had been established in England in the 19th century with the increase in the literacy rate of the working class. New media forms developed and expanded from this period onwards, but newspapers were always a central experience by which football followers absorbed their facts and myths of the game for generations. By the mid-1950s British people read more daily newspapers than any other nation in the world, an astonishing 615 per 1,000 doing so. These forms of blanket coverage were brought about by technological developments that could ensure that every corner of the nation could share in a specific experience. This reach was further enhanced by the introduction and widespread expansion of radio in the interwar period. The radio was the key instrument to domesticate a considerable section of the nation's leisure and entertainment, and football was part of this process. Matches would now be experienced by different groups interpreting events through different forms – the live crowd and the radio audience, beholden to the voice and skills of the commentator to implant a picture of events. Radio was the vehicle for the redirecting of a great amount of mass entertainment towards the home environment and away from the public arena. Of course radio offered a level of immediacy that the newspapers, even the post-match *Pink Finals* and *Green 'Uns* could not compete with. Radio and later reel films and television crystallised football and other sports into a structure that made the nation real and tangible through events and ceremonies endlessly repeated with imagery and symbolism drenching on to the enclosed scenes and relayed and interpreted by and to audiences both live and remote.

However, though the game and its reporting expanded exponentially, there had been tensions from the beginning of the founding of the Football League in 1887. From this point forward the players who would represent the national team were primarily contracted to individual clubs. The ongoing tetchy, testy and sometimes explosive relationship between the Football League and Football Association saw a core focus in the exhausting club versus country debate. The cycle of xenophobia and sometimes outright detestation of all things foreign continued over time with both football authorities competing to see who could be the most insular and condescending to anyone outside the British Isles who kicked a football.

One of the most eminent British football writers over many decades, Geoffrey Green, described British relations with FIFA between 1904 and 1952 as a halting story. Green is being somewhat generous in his conclusion. Perhaps a more accurate assessment would be to parallel FA and FIFA relations during that period to that of military conflict in the ancient Greek world, where there were sporadic outbreaks of peace in a near-permanent state of war. The arrogance and aloofness of the Football Association repeated itself in a never-ending echo, the desire for the British to abstain from continental involvement and interference into anything decided on the Sceptred Isle.

On two separate occasions the FA removed itself from membership of FIFA, which meant that for the 42 years of possible interaction between 1904 and 1946 the English association spent far more years outside the international fold than within it. Fundamentally, European international football did not take place during the period of the Great War. In the aftermath of hostilities ending FIFA wanted to bring back a sense of normality and invited the associations of Germany and Austria to rejoin the realm of international competition. The FA objected and promptly withdrew membership. After a hiatus membership was reluctantly re-established until 1926 when a longer breach took place over definitions of amateurism and the specific issue of broken-time payments. There was very little negotiation or appreciation of other viewpoints as the FA withdrew into a form of splendid isolation.

The broken time issue developed during the Congress of Rome in 1926 and drew in wider issues of discontent. The interpretation of broken time payments was down to individual associations and in accordance they interpreted the issue differently. The FA were also concerned to stop any interference by FIFA into the internal control and decision-making of a national association. The FA felt it was, at least partly, their position to dictate to the world governing body whether they could involve themselves in advice or procedure with one of their constituent members. Paramount among the FA's concerns with FIFA's involvement was that there was to be no changing of the laws of the game. The laws, according to the FA, were sacrosanct and carved deeper into stone than the tablets Moses brought down from Mount Sinai. In reality the rules and codes of football had been subtly and regularly altered since the 1860s. It was not the case that an original set of rules conceived in a singular meeting had remained untouched for 60 years.

Association football was not alone in splits over the definition of amateurism and in many sports, such as rugby union and athletics, inconsistency and conflict existed over many decades. However, it was the core value point that the FA chose to initiate their removal from being involved with an organisation which they had paid lip service to and found no beneficial reasons to remain within. This was a fateful decision which almost completely removed English involvement in European and world developments. The moat was deepened, the drawbridge pulled up and the portcullis slammed down to focus on the annual England v Scotland matches and the weekly happenings of matches in Stoke, Huddersfield and Sunderland.

It was 20 years before England rejoined and engaged with FIFA with a more internationalist outlook. This was in no short measure due to the efforts of one man – Stanley Rous. As Willy Meisl, a man never short of an opinion, stated in *World Sports Magazine* from November 1954, Britain's two-decades-long isolation had led to a virtual exclusion from the blood circulation of international soccer. These interwar developments did not just include the original invitational World Cup of 1930 and the expanding, European-based World Cups of 1934 and 1938, but such tournaments as the Mitropa Cup. The Mitropa Cup was founded in 1927 by Willy Meisl's brother Hugo and was competed for by the best club teams in Austria, Hungary, Italy, Yugoslavia and Czechoslovakia. Clearly English clubs could not have competed directly in this competition, but it was indicative of a broadening of the competitive base which English clubs were removed from.

Though England were not members of FIFA for most of the interwar period they did play matches, all friendlies, on the continent. A total of 23 were played by England in Europe between 1929 and 1939. With the four home nations rejoining, and crucially, remaining in FIFA, from 1947, it opened the door for regular competitive matches against elite European countries and later a smaller number of games against the powerhouses of South American football – Argentina, Brazil and Uruguay.

During this immediate postwar period England had a superb array of individual talent that overrode any issues around tactical awareness. This was never more apparent than in the incredible game against Portugal in 1947, specially arranged to celebrate the official opening of the Stadium of Light in Lisbon, where England destroyed their hosts 10-0. In one of Billy Wright's multiple autobiographies, *Football is My Passport*, there is a superb photograph which encapsulates the confidence of the English team. In many respects it is a standard photo of a pre-match line-up, but in reality it tells us so much more. The match in question was a zenith performance. A 10-0 away victory in European international football belongs to an era of clear disparity, to an age long lost, and is only replicated today against the minnows of San Marino or Andorra.

Perhaps in this photograph we have the greatest line-up England ever produced. The legendary names override any concerns for systems or tactics. The warmth and bright light shine out from the photograph with the England players all having rolled up the sleeves on their shirts to above the elbow.

Their perfect white shirts, expansively opened at the collar, are unfettered by any form of colouring or advertising, with just the large badge of the three lions over the left breast. The forward line of Matthews, Mannion, Mortensen, Lawton and Finney exude a relaxed and confident countenance. A packed stand fills the background. Goalkeeper Frank Swift looks slightly away at an angle, but most of the team look directly to the camera. It appears that in their minds they know they are going to destroy the opposition. How could you not be confident you would win comfortably with that forward line and Swift, Scott, Franklin and Wright behind?

However, only nine days previously England had suffered a 1-0 defeat to Switzerland which brought out a myriad of excuses from various quarters. In *The Stanley Matthews Story* the star winger stated that the main reason England lost this particular match was the size of the stadium and pitch. Matthews was unequivocal, 'A small ground doesn't suit an English international team. We are used to playing on spacious ones. On the small grounds the Swiss teams use, English players are apt to get a feeling of being closed in and playing on top of each other.' Matthews was informing us that this defeat in Zurich didn't really count as the home team had not obliged their opponents by selecting a pitch which was to their advantage.

Matthews was more concerned that the pitch's size affected his game and performance; with wing play compressed on a smaller and narrower surface the impact of line-hugging individuals was diminished. The question of whether England had adapted play, system or shape was not raised as a logical response to changing circumstances. The pitch and ground were the wrong size for England's one-dimensional approach. Dennis Brailsford, in *British Sport: A Social History*, describes football reeling from England's unthinkable defeat to Switzerland and a similar result for Scotland against Belgium, but the Switzerland defeat was repackaged with no inquiry or inquest. The excuses were made, and football moved on to the next game, which in this case was the aforementioned victory in Lisbon.

To celebrate the new union of England, Scotland, Wales and Northern Ireland being a full and active part of the wider football world, a major match was proposed. In fact, it was a monumental game in which, for the first time, a united British team took on the Rest of Europe. The match was held at Hampden Park in Glasgow, still the world's largest capacity football stadium in 1947. The combined talents of Swift, Ron Burgess, Matthews, Lawton and Billy Liddell swept aside Europe 6-1. Surely there was nothing to worry about from Europe with a result such as that. The *Daily Express* proclaimed the British team 'The Bosses of Soccer' and why would any of the 135,000 people watching the match conclude anything different? In other aspects of the game too this was a Golden Age. Attendances at English club matches reached their absolute peak in the late 1940s. Many crowds were simply restricted by the stadium capacity. In 1946/47 35.5 million people attended matches and this rose to the all-time high of 41.25 million in 1948/49.

A scratch Great Britain team playing a scratch European team was one thing, but now England were to start playing European nations on a more regular basis. There was no European Nations Cup until 1960 and FIFA rather generously allowed the British Home International Championship to double up as qualification for the 1950 World Cup finals held in Brazil. However, England playing a broader range of internationals brought a new range of tests not faced before. In addition to the Great Britain team match of 1947 there were the two, previously mentioned, widely differing results for the England team in that year which set a confusing pattern of positives and negatives. England attempted to deal with brilliant players, coached teams and differing systems as the proclaimed masters found out there were other approaches to the Beautiful Game.

England's first major test of genuine world football came in their appearance at the 1950 World Cup. This tournament provided a whole range of challenges and issues for which the FA party was completely unprepared. It also produced a match forever remembered by England fans with a shudder of incomprehension even at 70 years removed but had a different set of conclusions in 1950. When is a calamity not a calamity? When no one notices or gives a shit or every single excuse in the book is utilised to explain away the inexplicable. So it was with the performance of the England national team at the fourth World Cup, their first, and in particular the 1-0 defeat to the USA on 29 June 1950. The scene of this extraordinary result was Belo Horizonte, Brazil. In England's 1,000-plus full internationals this remains and almost certainly will always remain their worst result. The self-proclaimed supreme team, self-appointed favourites to win the tournament, were defeated by a genuine rag-tag and bobtail outfit who gave themselves so little chance of winning that they, allegedly, went out on the bevvy the night before.

Stanley Matthews epitomised the confused and illogical stance of this period. He stated before the 1950 finals, 'It looks like a piece of cake for England to win the World Cup.' This was despite the tournament being played in a country England had never played an international in before, in fact in a continent they'd never played an international in before. Even though the England players knew nothing of their opponents in Pool 2 – Chile, Spain and the USA. Despite all these overriding factors, Matthews still concluded after watching Brazil defeat Mexico 4-0 that England would win the tournament. Preparation was an alien concept to the FA party in Brazil with decisions and non-decisions reaching farcical levels. There were some voices, Stanley Rous and Walter Winterbottom, attempting a broader approach and vision, but their outlook was not shared by too many of those directly involved in the tournament.

A major contributor to the recorded memory of the USA match is England captain Billy Wright. The producer of four autobiographies during his playing career, Wright covered the defeat in considerable detail in both *The World's My Football Pitch* (1953) and *Football is My Passport* (1957) where he laid down the points and arguments that became the gospel for all following generations of England fans and commentators. Coached in the casual racism of the 1950s, Wright was clearly no fan of Brazil as a country, or Brazilians – it wasn't Ironbridge. He described the whole Brazilian experience as a pain in the neck. In the saccharine sweet and anodyne world of 1950s footballers' autobiographies this is about as strong as it gets. Clearly, he hated the whole experience.

Wright offered a wide range of reasons why England flopped, as he termed it, at the 1950 World Cup. The USA game appeared to offer a form of template to try and excuse every team's defeat before or since. In general terms the two group defeats were due to the plethora of missed chances by the strikers (a beautiful dumping of responsibility for defeat on to attack from defence, as Matthews would later reverse responsibility for the 6-3 defeat), the humidity of Brazil which made breathing difficult and led to a negative effect on players' stamina, the thick grass of the pitches which was unusual for the England players and the complete change of diet which created the 'Rio stomach'. So somehow one of the reasons for England being defeated by the USA was Brazilian people cooking Brazilian dishes in a Brazilian manner, which affected some of the players. It was perceived as the responsibility of the Brazilian hotel staff to prepare British meals without any previous experience of cooking such food. It wasn't the responsibility of the touring party and FA management to have thought about, planned and prepared for this issue in a party of 30 in Brazil for potentially three or four weeks. These points create a framework for excusing poor results, with differing aspects all neatly covered – team-mates, pitch, the foreign nature of everything and the weather. Wright then moves to the USA game specifically.

In an enhanced batch of contributory factors there were the inadequate changing facilities, which led to interference from Walter Winterbottom and the team changing at a local sports club. For Wright the forward line was clearly to blame as they had a dozen chances where the ball did not run for England and end up in their opponents' net. Two more excuses followed – one the oldest in the game of football and the other an unusual message which became core in concluding this defeat as being in some way invalid. In a single sentence Wright connected this match with thousands that went before and after, 'Some of the poorest refereeing I have ever seen gave the Americans more than their share of good fortune.' Every follower can understand the captain here. Even though virtually no fans travelled from England to see the game, we all know that at the very least the man in black had the eyesight of Mr Magoo. The second of the reasons was far more unusual and in 1950 was, perhaps, a difficult one for the English football public to take on board. This was the legal validity of several of the American team for even being on the pitch. Not only had England lost to Johnny Foreigner but there were incorrect foreigners in the team. The goalscorer Gaetjens was Haitian and there was a Scot lurking in the team too, an ex-Wrexham player. The negativity and endless excuses continued with Wright not being able to give Gaetjens any credit for his match-winning goal. It was a stone-cold fluke. According to Wright the ball just hit the back of his head as he attempted to duck under the ball and the deflection threw the goalkeeper, Bert Williams. Further flukes followed with the USA goalkeeper making numerous saves with his face. The goal was not even a real goal scored by someone who shouldn't have been on a pitch that was cut at the wrong length for England in a stadium that wasn't up to scratch in a country that was humid and foreign.

All players and supporters develop their safety net of excuses for defeats as soon as they are involved in the game. From the most crazed eye-popping ultra to almost every manager ever to screaming, hyper-ventilating South American commentators to seven-year-olds just starting their playing and supporting journey, we all do it. A never-ending, always-increasing list of excuses for defeat – ranging from the totally logical to the surreal. From our own personal database of excuses, we will bring forth a selection to explain away in our own minds the defeat of the team we were playing for or watching. We couldn't possibly have been beaten by our opponents because on the day they played better than us and took their chances and deserved to win. The endless flow from our own personal filing cabinets all on immediate standby to explain our own or our team's inadequacies – it was too hot, too cold, too muddy, too waterlogged, grassless pitch, bone-hard pitch, biased referee, corrupt referee and linesman, injuries, lucky goalkeeper, fluke goalkeeping performance, deflection, rain, snow, mist, sleet, hail, wrong kit, wrong boots, intimidating crowd or stadium, poor preparation, poor hotel, poor changing facilities, poor transport to ground, poor fans, no fans, aggressive fans, too much atmosphere, no atmosphere, incorrect offside decision, cheating and blatant fouls not given – all add to the mix to create a scandal of Watergate proportions against you or your team.

Alf Ramsey, who played in this game, was of a slightly different opinion as he claimed to be of the view that the USA were never going to be a pushover. He felt that on the decent surface of the Belo Horizonte pitch the USA were a good team, with Ed de Souza and Eddy McIllvenny both having particularly good games. David Winner, writing 55 years later, held the exact opposite opinion, stating that the USA were genuine no-hopers who had lost 9-0 to Italy in a World Cup warm-up game, only emphasising that England's defeat was, using Brian Glanville's word, cataclysmic. Winner retrospectively connected this defeat with Winston Churchill's claim that the few years after World War Two marked the greatest fall in the rank and stature of Britain in the world since the loss of the American colonies 200 years previously. However, although USA had lost their first game at the tournament 3-1 to Spain, they had actually taken the lead and held on to it until just ten minutes remained.

All these excuses and negative comments created a web of non-responsibility. The defeat was due to a vast range of factors, most of which were beyond the influence of the FA or any of the players on the pitch. Wright's advice for England to improve and, fundamentally, compete at world level was not to look forward but to look back, in a similar vein to Matthews. Wright argued that the future of the game in England was to return to an Excalibur-wielding mythical age where all opponents were dispatched to the sword. His concluding statement of a call to arms was so vague it's very difficult to unpack what is actually being argued, 'The sooner we in Britain return to the old teachings the better it will be for our footballers. The game as a whole … we in this island are capable of producing the best football in the world, providing all connected with the great game are prepared to put everything they possess in to achieving this end.'

Wright's autobiographies came out as regular as clockwork throughout his playing career, and as previously mentioned, *The World's My Football Pitch* (1953) was followed four years later by *Football is My Passport*. In some areas his outlook of the world game became a little bit more sophisticated but in others it remained an *idée fixe*. In his 1953 version of a world XI (and two substitutes) the result was overwhelmingly insular with nine Englishmen, two Welshmen and a Scot present and only one foreign player – Gerhard Hanappi of Austria. There was no room for Ferenc Puskás, Nándor Hidegkuti or Alfredo Di Stéfano. However, the four-year gap and two defeats to Hungary and the 1954 Switzerland World Cup had not altered his fundamental range of factors for defeat to the USA. In fact, a few new ones were added for good measure – bone-hard pitches, all five England forwards had an off-day together, and Gaetjens' goal was now relegated to the level of being the freakiest goal Wright witnessed in his entire career. Only on one occasion did Wright complement the United States for their victory, in the form of player Ed de Souza, who he rated as a quality player with the skill and football brain to unlock the England defence. Apart from this one positive comment on the USA team Wright's negative diatribe continued with further lamentations on the attributes of the referee, whose performance was now concluded as extraordinary. Wright was not at any point concerned about tactics or systems. The focus was to package and explain away this defeat as a fluke that was due to a totally bizarre combination of factors including the weather and preparation of the opposition, all of which were completely beyond the remit of the FA party and players.

The other England player on the pitch in Belo Horizonte and later at the Hungary game, to comment considerably in a contemporary autobiography, was Alf Ramsey. Ramsey was, perhaps, the most nationalistic Englishman who ever walked the earth, so it is no surprise that his view of the USA defeat was even more lacking in balance than Wright's. In the rather slim at 110 pages *Talking Football*, published by the stalwarts of sporting biographies Stanley Paul, Ramsey took us through a fabulous list of mistakes and blatantly unfair scenarios leading to the US defeat. He stated that in training matches he was already finding it very hard to breathe. The humidity or altitude clearly had a negative effect on Ramsey as he argued he felt infinitely more tired after an easy kickabout than after a hectic league match.

In complete contradiction to Matthews' statement that England would, basically, walk the 1950 World Cup, Ramsey stated that he never thought it was going to be easy against the USA. Ramsey brought forward a range of factors, mostly echoing those of Wright. The stadium was not complete with inadequate changing facilities. He equated the stadium to playing in a prison with a crowd that was totally hostile to the England team and enthusiastically supported the USA and reiterated the central point that several of the USA team were not qualified to play in the match. Ramsey then beautifully manoeuvred the result to one of English largesse, 'A player can only play in a World Cup for the country for which he is qualified by birth, so England, if they had felt that way, could have lodged a protest against the USA, but that is not our way of going about things.'

An England team containing some of the greatest players ever to wear the shirt may have lost to a raggle-taggle bunch of disparate semi-professionals, but the moral, almost imperial, high ground was retained. Ramsey encapsulated the tsunami of excuses after offering up the beautiful riposte of 'I'm not making excuses, but' – all tied up in a bow to bring forth every excuse possible including a year's bad luck in the first half, the USA goalkeeper stopping multiple shots with his face, Gaetjens' goal was a one-in-a-million freak, Mortensen having a goal disallowed and the superhuman efforts of the England team going unrewarded.

The construct of the Belo Horizonte myth was complete. The core issue was that almost no England supporters travelled to Brazil to see the game live and there was no cinema film or British television coverage. The events as laid down by the likes of Wright and Ramsey became the absolute truth for generations of fans and followers from 1950 onwards. In his 2003 autobiography Tom Finney recalled that the English press had a field day with an inquest that ran and ran. However, the reality was somewhat more complex, and the construct of the fluke was laid on this result, which excused any need to change approach in a deeper manner.

The game was in a tournament new to most British football fans, in a city most had never heard of, in a country almost no British people had visited. The tumult of excuses, factors and reasons brought forward meant the whole match was placed in a drawer marked 'embarrassing defeat – fluke'. Of course, not everyone in the small group of players and observers was motivated by trying to get this game brushed under the carpet. For some journalists present the USA defeat represented more. However, they were very much in a minority as their sports editors concentrated on other parallel sporting calamities, notably the England cricket team's defeat to the West Indies in a Test match. Amazingly, when the footballers returned from Brazil there was only one reporter at the airport to interview Billy Wright and the myth-laying process began from this point.

Leo McKinstry viewed the defeat to the USA in catastrophic terms and he, surely, was correct to describe it as the greatest upset in the nation's sporting history, a record almost certainly never to be touched unless San Marino win 3-0 one day at Wembley. McKinstry claimed it haunted the players involved for years afterwards and was always a stain on their reputations. Perhaps that is correct and that was always the main motivation for the approach of the likes of Wright and Ramsey. McKinstry's other central contention that England had been turned into an international laughing stock was somewhat more complicated. All sporting performances and results are relative, and England were not alone in a poor or even disastrous World Cup. Brian Glanville ranked the three other pre-tournament favourites as Brazil, Italy and Sweden. Sweden made it to the final pool and were then beaten by Uruguay and lost 7-1 to Brazil. Italy were knocked out at the same stage as England and Brazil suffered their psychological catastrophe of defeat in the final match against Uruguay, which caused years of existential torment. For various differing reasons Germany, Argentina, Hungary, Scotland, France, Czechoslovakia and Austria weren't even there.

A point often downplayed or ignored is that after this defeat England still had an opportunity to qualify for the final pool phase by beating Spain. The match took place just two days later but also ended in a 1-0 defeat and England were on their way home – immediately. The thorough inquest and assessment did not take place and the party started their mythologising from the moment Billy Wright spoke to the single reporter as he got off the plane. The relentless nature of professional football, as so brilliantly detailed in *Red or Dead* by David Peace, meant that even in 1950 there was the switch to cricket, players' holidays, pre-season training and then the undisputed focus on the 42-game league season for Blackpool and Bolton, Tottenham and Arsenal. The players, of course, had a lot of motivation to deflect, downplay or blame someone or something else and move on swiftly to the opening game of the 1950/51 domestic season. We've all cocked up at work and used those two key tactics – blame someone else or try to minimise the damage by never even mentioning the issue. Footballers went to work, and their work was professional football. In certain respects they were no different from anyone else.

The inquest may have been shelved for most people but for those with a bigger perspective they took some underlying factors from the 1950 World Cup. England had lost two games out of three in a group that looked straightforward enough in a depleted tournament. Stanley Rous had commented that the USA had seemed 'fitter, faster and better fighters', but this was just a general comment on the gap in preparation between England and other teams. From kit to diet to selection process, England had bordered on a joke. While Brazil racked up astonishing score after astonishing score with their plethora of coaches, dieticians and a psychologist, England had Arthur Drewry, the Grimsby fishmonger, as their sole selector present in Brazil. The team was only exclusively selected by the manager when Alf Ramsey took the post and he made that a core condition of accepting the job. In the long reign of Walter Winterbottom the team was chosen by the international selection committee. Over the 1950s and early 1960s Winterbottom increased his voice on this archaic process, but in 1950 the committee chose the team and the coach got on with it. The committee brought a short-term outlook, ego, localised agendas of members pushing players from their own club and 'flavours of the month' appearing from nowhere for one or two caps and then being cast into oblivion if they weren't Steve Bloomer, Raich Carter and Stanley Matthews rolled into one.

When the 1950 World Cup debacle was over for England after their defeat to Spain there was very little desire for almost any of the FA party to stay in Brazil for one minute more than was necessary. Wright and Matthews both claimed that they wanted to stay to watch the final stages of the tournament, but they were informed that everyone was to return to the UK together. The longer-term problem for England was that the tournament performances could be swept under the carpet and there was a quick move to business as usual. There was no deep or wide-reaching inquiry to assess England's performances or to investigate areas for improvement.

One major development that did come forward from the dual force of Rous and Winterbottom was the ad hoc expansion of international opponents, up to the November 1953 match against Hungary. Historically England had played a surfeit of matches against Scotland, Wales, Ireland, Northern Ireland and the Republic of Ireland. With the clear exception of Scotland, it was annual matches against Wales and the Irelands which gave England such a strong win ratio. The expansion of European opponents involved games against a disproportionally small number of countries – France, Belgium and Austria. From 1950 onwards England started to regularly play other European nations and there was further expansion to start playing matches against the major South American countries – Argentina and Uruguay in 1953 and Brazil in 1956. In the three years between the

USA defeat and the 6-3 Hungary match England played Yugoslavia, Argentina, Portugal, France, Austria, Italy, Switzerland, Belgium, Chile, Uruguay, USA and the FIFA Rest of Europe team.

The evolutionary process after the 1950 World Cup was glacial, not revolutionary. The split of football in England was clear during this period with those wanting to hitch a ride on the new ideas coming through doing so and those who didn't continuing to exist in their self-defined bubble and excusing or ignoring failures and shortcomings. The two main drivers of development – Rous and Winterbottom – implemented an FA technical subcommittee to try and assess what was required to improve English football in the competitive international arena. Several club chairmen, international players, managers and some press met and had some limited input, but core issues such as team selection by the international committee were not forcefully challenged.

The committee asked a myriad of voices for their opinion on how to progress and, unsurprisingly, they got a myriad of responses. The position of coaching remained controversial at the elite end of English football. There were calls for advanced training for internationals which juxtaposed against the widely held view that coaching was overvalued to the detriment of match practice. The endless obsession with the club v country argument reared its Medusa's head with a focus on the conflict between international and league football. There continued to be an appreciation by clusters of minds of the riches of the world game in Rio de Janeiro, Buenos Aires, Montevideo, Vienna and Budapest, but they acted as islands of interest and knowledge. The real tragedy of the World Cup in 1950 is that England lost to the USA and that game could be packaged as a fluke, that they weren't played off the park by Brazil or Uruguay. The power and influence of the apologists remained for this reason. One of the few concrete implementations was the introduction of 'B' internationals, though their importance and relevance to developing a top-class international side can clearly be questioned.

There were new and challenging experiences for England during the period of 1950 to 1953. These matches should have shown to everyone not necessarily England's inferiority or set ways but, that there were approaches across Europe and South America which had other stories to tell. Three important components consistently written about by commentators contemporary and secondary are the 1951 home draw against Austria, the 1953 tour of South America and, rather bizarrely, the 4-4 draw with the FIFA Rest of Europe team four weeks before the Hungary game in 1953.

Austria had long been a focus of football development. The bigger sister to Budapest in a *Mitteleuropa* hub of ideas and discussion of the game involving some of the greatest football coaching and management brains – Béla Guttmann, Hugo Meisl and Gusztáv Sebes. The interwar Austrian *Wunderteam* was long gone, swallowed up in the Nazi stroll across the border that was the Anschluss. However, the team of the early 1950s were held as one of the strongest on the continent. England played Austria twice in six months, in late 1951 at Wembley and in May 1952 in Vienna. In his *Talking Football*, Alf Ramsey interestingly pointed out that the Wembley-based 'Match of the Century' Austrian version was attended by many English professional players who were there to pick up tips, in a precursor to the galaxy of future important managers and coaches who attended the 6-3 game. Some professionals were clearly interested in viewing different teams, systems and approaches. Indeed, this was only the second non-British and Irish team to play a full international at Wembley.

Brian Glanville saw Austria as the pre-eminent European side who had developed after the 1950 World Cup, with their star performer Ernst Ocwirk. The master British football writer viewed this match as another clear clash of football styles and culture. England rolled out their 'normal' game, with a 'dogged, uninspired, uncoordinated attack and a defence which persistently fell back before Austrian attacks'. This was the straightforward tactic of retreating defence. Geoffrey Green went further, interpreting the season of 1951/52 as the year of real awakening in terms of international football. He defined the Austria match as one of the truly great ones. England took the challenge seriously enough to arrange specific training at Maine Road, Manchester City's ground, in what Green termed an unprecedented step. Though after this level of preparation there was the oft-repeated issue of injuries that meant Billy Wright was not utilised in a new role in attack as a 'loose' forward but was retained at wing-half and Stan Mortensen was withdrawn.

The selection panel decided to award first caps to Ivor Broadis and Arthur Milton. Green was under no illusion that this was a scratch England team. The importance of the 2-2 draw is placed in a global context of retaining England's unbeaten home record, for one more match at least. Green acknowledged that it was a close thing with Austria's skilled ball players who exhibited energy, a smart approach to the game and, the writer perceived, with a combination short and long passing game, the Austrians possessed a deeper knowledge of the game than England. Other contemporary commentators on the match included stalwart journalist Ivan Sharpe in *40 Years of Football*. Sharpe went back to pre-World War Two analysis, being present in a myriad of situations from audiences with Benito Mussolini and the Italian World Cup winners of 1934 to being privy to secret information from former Burnley player and referee Charles Sutcliffe during the Pools War of 1936.

International selection games have always held a strange position in how much attention is given to them. Of course, it's exciting for fans and commentators to experience these dream teams, but what real relevance do they have? Gusztáv Sebes, Hungary's coach, was clear that the October 1953 match between England and the FIFA Select XI had no relevance whatsoever. He refused to release any of his players for the fixture as he didn't wish to pander to the egos of a few high-ranking FIFA and FA officials. The purity of the game shone through for Sebes.

The amazing thing about this fantasy game is how much was written about it, both at the time and down the decades, and how much store was put on both result and performance to a level not replicated in other select internationals. When Great Britain had dispatched FIFA in 1947 it was seen in Britain as confirming that the old order reigned. The England v FIFA match in 1963 and even the bizarre sight of seeing Tommy Smith lining up for Team America v England in 1976 never got anything like the same attention as the 1953 game. The FIFA team for that encounter was not a World XI but a completely Eurocentric side. There were no players from the current world champions, Uruguay, and neither Brazil nor Argentina. The FIFA team consisted of three Austrians, three Yugoslavs, two Spaniards, a West German, an Italian and a Swede. Players came from just six European nations with ex-Hungarian international László Kubala representing Spain in one of those fluid nationality decisions which sport deals so well in.

In response to this range of talent the England selection committee countered with experienced star players – Merrick, Ramsey, Eckersley, Wright, Dickinson, Matthews, Mortensen and Lofthouse formed the core of the team, but there were also a couple of selectors' specials in Ufton and Mullen. Derek Ufton, of Charlton Athletic, had the unenviable role of facing up to Europe's best strikers playing in a formation unfamiliar to most English destroyers. Without any sense of irony Ufton stated that it had been impossible in two days of preparation for him to understand how the rest of the team played and how to react to them. Of course, Ufton played against all those players every season. The team that had very little preparation and had to deal with additional complexities such as language barriers and formation disparities were their opponents.

Ufton struggled in the FIFA match to pick up and deal with Gunnar Nordahl who was playing a more withdrawn role. Bill Eckersley was reputedly furious at the positional confusion and at half-time berated other defenders. Winterbottom tried to defuse the situation by talking to Ufton and agreeing that the approach in the first half wasn't working and that the revised plan would be to let Nordahl go, stay back and seal the central defensive area. Poor old Ufton was held responsible for the poor performance of the English defence that day and his showing against the combined talents of some of the world's best players was to be his one and only England cap. Here was the reality of England's national team in their final match at Wembley before hosting Hungary 35 days later.

Context: English Society 1945–1953

THE PERIOD from the end of World War Two to the early 1950s was one of an ever-changing process as Britain's role in the world altered, even if many were deeply reluctant to acknowledge that such a process had begun. England was in a crux, caught between the old world of the interwar period and the newer world of full employment and the material advancements this brought. Connectivity with other nations was also changing in context and practicality, in football as in other social aspects. The Little Englander was and remained for many decades a constant image of the England football supporter, but the national team by the first half of the 1950s was beginning a process of engagement – the 1950 and 1954 World Cups, Argentina playing at Wembley, the 1953 summer tour of South America and in November 1953 the Hungarians arrived.

During World War Two planning had entered the British lexicon as civil society was turned into a production process for total, immersive war. A *laissez-faire* approach had taken a back seat and once Clement Attlee's Labour government was returned in 1945 planning continued a central position and pace. Planning was a concept that had a slow introduction to English football with all the expected doubters and negative commentators, but the overall concept of planning was a core tenet of British government between 1945 to 1953 and its prevalence in an intellectual context was paramount. The new planning structures had a deep impact on major areas of British life and showed that with a new approach of co-ordination and a centralised planning process, considerable improvements could be achieved.

The Poor Law was abolished and replaced by a wide range of new structures – a free National Health Service, a comprehensive national insurance programme, grants were provided for university students and in areas such as the 1947 Town and Country Planning Act there was an introduction of planning controls into the physical fabric of both urban and rural Britain. In a three-year stretch in the immediate postwar period there was a wide-reaching process of nationalisation of key industries and services – 1946 banking, 1947 communications and coal, 1948 electricity and transport and 1949 gas. It was in the middle of this programme that Stanley Rous introduced and implemented his reconstruction plan for football. The focus for Rous was that improvement in the English game would benefit from systematic planning in numerous areas. Rous brought forward a comprehensive set of ideas – the FA should publish its own periodical and a management textbook and training to equip players for their later working lives. Rous was keen on improving communication in the game, to expand the role of coaching which formed a consistent place from 1948 onwards in the annual *FA Book for Boys*.

Though it was a Labour government that initiated the sweeping economic and social changes, the programme did not stop when a Winston Churchill-led Conservative government took office in 1951. The postwar political consensus was established. There were five main themes

38

where Labour and the Conservatives adopted a similar approach – full employment was accepted as a central aim, the involvement of trade unions by consultation, respect for the welfare state, the fundamentals of defence, foreign and imperial policy shared common ground and the development of a mixed economy with an increased state sector.

These fundamental changes to British society brought about considerable improvement in the lives of working-class people. The welfare state's growth gave everyone free access to secondary education and healthcare and a growing economic security enabled individuals and families to plan for their own futures. People could afford to enjoy the present with a confidence that lives and experiences would improve over time. The increase in confidence and almost full employment brought a rise in material consumption. Credit facilities widened for many in the working classes, who responded by acquiring a galaxy of consumer goods – fridges, cookers, televisions, three-piece suites, cars, vacuum cleaners, washing machines and the introduction of convenience food. This was a world away from the experiences of the depression and mass unemployment in the interwar period.

The increase in consumerism was connected to an increase in free time. Consumer culture continued to develop at pace in the 1950s with an equal expansion in the consumption of services as well as goods through the mass market. The commercialisation and consumption of sport was nothing new, but the specific patterns represented by a consumer culture and the manner in which sports were associated with it expanded during this period.

In a domestic political and social context, growth and improvement were clear. The frequently voiced concept of declinism was used more appropriately in the international context. The British working class looked inward to its own cultures both new and established. Through consumerism and the rise of leisure time the experience landscape was altered for those who wanted it altered.

Television became a national social phenomenon. The reduced costs of a once introductory product brought its acquisition to mass levels. The early 1950s saw the beginning of the explosion in the ownership of television, from tens of thousands of sets in 1950 to four million in 1955 and then to ten million in 1960, bringing about a visual interpretation and update to the aural presence of the wireless. A homogeneity of culture pervaded with newly televisually aware households from Plymouth to Newcastle sharing in national experiences in equal measure.

A part of this expanded national culture and a repetitive national calendar was sport, including a central position for football. Football flowed as a core part of this created and re-emphasised national sporting calendar, driven by the developments in mass media creating a taut procession of nationally covered events from January to December, repeated annually, creating an endless stream of winners and losers, heroes and villains. This annual journey started with rugby union's Five Nations Championship, the varsity boat race, the Grand National, the FA Cup Final, Test match cricket, the Derby, Wimbledon, the Open and the commencement of the Football League season. By the early 1950s this cycle was deeply embedded in the culture of different social classes. The internalising of British society can clearly be seen in the homogeneity of these events. There were some foreign competitors in this fabric, but it was overwhelmingly an intra-island experience. British competitors at British venues, watched by British crowds live and absorbed through British media by millions of Britons.

So 1953 was a key year in this development with the tense and exciting FA Cup Final of Blackpool's victory over Bolton Wanderers (the 'Matthews Final') and then the 6-3 loss to Hungary in November. In all the post-match analysis of the Hungarians' victory on that dreary day, a point that is often overlooked is that the game was on the cusp of television coverage of football. Followers of the sport across the country could now see, assess and judge for themselves a player's or a team's performance. Francois Bedarida termed the *homo Britannicus* pastime of watching television as an absolute revolution which turned the open-air sportsman into a stay-at-home *homo televidens*. The urban, working-class male, who provided the core football follower, had increased options for how to spend his leisure time, along with an increased awareness of other football worlds. Through match coverage genuine stars were born and sustained whether they were British – Matthews, Finney or Liddell – or from further afield in Puskás, Hidegkuti or Di Stéfano.

Football in Britain was previously experienced by either walking through the turnstile to watch the match live or tuning in on the wireless and constructing the game in your head. In the first half of the 1950s, with increased consumer spending and technological advances, this all changed. Though Wembley was rammed with 100,000 supporters in November 1953 it was still a fraction of those who would watch those Hungarian players flitting about the pitch bringing defeat to England. Television in a wealthy country, such as Britain, brought a new vision of global football and the best teams of the decade – Hungary, Brazil, Uruguay and later Real Madrid – and the concept of global players such as Puskás, Garrincha and Pelé.

In contrast to domestic material improvements, nowhere was the perceived issue of declinism more debated than in the area of nationalism and imperialism. Commentators both contemporary and secondary have repeatedly connected performances of the English national football team with their views of Britain as a declining international power in political, economic and military terms. The empire was running on fumes but in 1953 it was still a vast global entity encompassing hundreds of millions of people. In 1953 only a small number of nation states had thrown off the oppressive British control – most notably India and Pakistan in 1947, followed the next year by Burma and Ceylon. There was no sudden, overnight collapse of the empire and in the first half of the 1950s the main phase of decolonisation was a full decade away when states all over Africa and Asia removed themselves from direct imperial control and the empire mutated into the Commonwealth. In the gap before the thorough dismantling of the empire and the loss of Cyprus, Sierra Leone, Uganda and other states the focus for foreign policy was the Cold War, the spread of communism and the rising ideological split across continental Europe.

Nationalism in football was a febrile, fluid process with changes in levels and specific hate teams. In the 1950s a more relaxed view persisted in terms of pent-up xenophobia (except perhaps in the mind of Alf Ramsey) to all and sundry. The major exception to this was the annual England v Scotland international which even by 1950 had had 80 years to fester and grow with dispute, in addition to the weight of actions at Culloden, Bannockburn and Flodden. England and Argentina's ongoing match-based disputes were not even an issue in the two completed internationals between the two countries by 1953.

Nationalism and imperialism were not such intense elements to the game in the 1950s. As previously recorded, the defeat to the USA had little overall impact with reporting fading away quite quickly after the 1950 World Cup was over. How could it be any different when all the English journalists who went to Brazil to cover the tournament returned on the same plane as the FA party? Indeed, we could conclude that patriotism rather than direct nationalism was more the norm in supporting and following England in the 1950s. The small coterie of journalists who travelled to Brazil were decidedly measured in their articles in comparison to the endless venom of a personal nature cascaded down on later England managers such as Bobby Robson and Graham Taylor. It was to Winterbottom's personal benefit in this area that the role and influence of the England coach was less influential and low-profile than in more recent decades. Nationalism in the media was written in a negative and derogatory context later as the full throttle of the empire breaking up hit home. The communist state and club sides had very little experience of playing British teams before 1953 with the British tour of Dynamo Moscow a fading memory of eight years previously. The dynamic of relations between the west of NATO and the east of the Warsaw Pact had altered radically between 1945 to 1953 with the Cold War across Europe and the Iron Curtain drawing its rigid line across the continent, defining a bipolar existence for decades.

In contrast to this reduced role internationally, change within Britain had many positives between 1945 and 1953. There was fundamentally more money and leisure time for many. Changes to working and living conditions brought new technologies, new work patterns, reduced working hours, increased average wages and statutory holiday rights which created the framework for existing leisure activities to expand and new leisure activities to take shape. By the mid-to-late 1950s British cultural commentators were concluding that fundamentally high and low culture had fused into one classless entity. Primary among these was Richard Hoggart who, in his 1957 work *The Uses of Literacy*, argued that this move to cultural classlessness was forged through sport, popular music, fiction, the media and holidays accessed and developed through the processes of uniformity and commercialisation. Hoggart somewhat milked the point by stating that the aristocracy and the working classes were sharing common experiences watching the same football matches and films and engaging in the newer social and non-social leisure activity of watching television.

Where Hoggart saw classlessness, the German Marxist theorist Karl Kautsky argued that even by the late 19th century it was organised professional sport that had deflected the British working class from their historic mission – devoting their material means and leisure time to football, horse racing and boxing – rather than absorbing the latest interpretations and analysis of the means of production. Marxist leisure theorists were later still going on about this in critical theory form. The Frankfurt School concluded that freedom in leisure was illusory. The capitalist society innately packaged, promoted and processed leisure for a mass market and mass appeal, in a similar manner to other commodities. There was no freedom of choice within the leisure markets.

The sporting contest is a constructed entity within time and space created by a set of arbitrary and sometimes bizarre rules. An imagined contest where all life and rules outside the enclosure of the contest can be suspended – where all the nonsense of anyone's life can be removed and forgotten. The perfect example of this suspension is boxing, where behaviour that in general society would result in involvement from the legal system, paradoxically can bring huge financial reward. Tony Collins in *Sport in Capitalist Society* perfectly encapsulated the debate of sport's depth of attraction by arguing that there were not imagined communities, to use Benedict Anderson's famous phrase, to those millions who attended sporting contests every week, but real ones. Real groups with their own shared memories, folklore and complex relationships revolving around class, regionalism and nationalism.

The Situation in 1953

MANY SUBSEQUENT commentators have interpreted England's 6-3 defeat of 1953 in the context of perceived negative events which followed in the mid-to-late 1950s – specifically the Suez Canal debacle of 1956 and the reduction of the British Empire. The early 1950s found Britain at the end of a 40-year period of tumult – the Great War and World War Two bookending the chaotic, depressive interwar period. By the early 1950s Britain had moved forward domestically, socially and economically. The major challenges were in foreign policy. The early and mid-1950s were a turning point in British society where the shadow of a war-based economy and the privations of rationing finally dissipated and were replaced by the long unattainable dreams of US-styled materialism. By the summer of 1954 the popular US magazine *Newsweek* reported avidly that the defined economic miracle of continental capitalist Europe had landed in Britain.

Changes also took place at the hierarchical pinnacle in 1952 when in February that year King George VI died. The reluctant and somewhat ill-equipped monarch, who did his duty in 1936 and provided a figurehead for the state and empire during the depths and then rejoices of World War Two, had passed the baton of monarchy to his young daughter

Elizabeth II. A positive interpretation of the beginning of her reign was encapsulated in the phrase, 'a second Elizabethan era'. Changes were afoot, distancing Britain of 1952 and 1953 from the prewar age. In March 1952 a major wartime restriction was abolished – the strongly disliked identity cards. In December of the same year a dense fog descended on London, forcing a stop to almost all transport and killing 4,000 people in the choking, toxic smog. Toxicity of a different type was released in October 1952 as Britain joined the USA and USSR in the club of nuclear weapons powers. It was at the Monte Bello Islands off Australia that Britain tested its first atomic bomb, unleashing not just the extreme power to vaporise a frigate placed close to the explosion, but a whole new sector of vocabulary was instantly utilised by football journalists nationwide. A nuclear capability reinforced Britain's need to remain seated at the top table of international relations. This belief that Britain was still up there punching with the bipolar superpowers seemed secure to many in 1953, but three years later it was destroyed as a fallacy after the Suez Crisis.

It was in 1953 that the path to confrontation in the Suez Canal was set, during that summer, when King Farouk of Egypt was forced to abdicate by the military, who then declared Egypt a republic. In October the following year Colonel Nasser rose to the top of the pile to take command of the state. In July 1956 Nasser declared that the Suez Canal was nationalised by the Egyptian government. The canal was not just about the practicality of monies received from charges or the assertion of nationhood, but a forceful contest against the ancient order of the European colonial powers and their dictatorial and excluding attitudes to the peoples of the Middle East. The military disaster which ensued for the British army, the lack of support from the United States and the ruination of the prime ministership of Anthony Eden signified the end of any role number one.

In a mirror image of the sharp realisation of the two defeats to Hungary in 1953 and 1954, the foreign policy of Britain would forever become second tier and a dictate of the United States. In a short period, the cloak of self-deceiving could only vanish in the wind and *realpolitik* present itself. Of course, for many it presented no such reality, but in the assessment of Francois Bedarida, Britain passed from being 'the smallest of the great powers' to the 'greatest of the small powers'. The declinist argument interpreted Suez as a crux point with the later decolonisation of Africa, the marginal role of the British in the Cold War with a series of spy-related embarrassments and Charles de Gaulle's veto on Britain joining the nascent EEC, all present in the repeated case for Britain becoming smaller and smaller on the world stage, in contrast to the clear rise in living standards of most Britons within the enclosed entity of the archipelago.

In the complex picture of the 1950s, achievement and disaster were key episodes such as the 1953 FA Cup Final, the conquest of Everest and Roger Bannister's sub-four-minute mile. These events were all seen as positive aspects of British achievement which cloaked the nation's sporting world in a protective armour, highlighting so many of the defined British attributes – determination, quiet success, modesty and plucky achievement. Everest had remained unconquered, due to the restrictions on foreigners entering Nepal, for decades. In 1953 the summit of the world's highest mountain was finally obtained for the pantheon of human achievement by a New Zealander and a Nepali. However, the victory of Everest was British-led and was communicated as such – British in the existential sense that anyone who was part of the empire and now the Commonwealth counted.

This was usually only a temporary arrangement and only for something positive. This gift of pseudo-Britishness was usually handed out to those of the former White Dominions – New Zealand among them. An official move was made to draw a veil over empire and give impetus to the new Commonwealth of Nations. Famously the news of this achievement broke on the day of Elizabeth II's coronation. *The Times* went somewhat over the top in connecting Everest and Francis Drake's circumnavigation of the planet and implicitly connecting the new reign of Elizabeth II to the long *Glorianna* of Elizabeth I.

The sporting rollercoaster of highs and lows continued into 1954. In the month of May were perhaps the two most extreme results imaginable. On the 23rd of that month England recorded their worst result statistically, being destroyed 7-1 in Budapest by Hungary's Mighty Magyars. Seventeen days earlier, a mythical barrier of human performance was eternally shattered as medical student Roger Bannister ran the world's first sub-four-minute mile. The true-blue students of Oxford flew the flag for amateurism in that seemingly endless tension between amateur and professional in English sport. Though the event, reported live on television, appeared low-key it was not amateurish in the sense of being haphazard. The rigorous training regime and the self-sacrifice of two Olympians, Christopher Brasher and Christopher Chataway, pacemaking for Bannister, led to his momentous time of three minutes and 59.6 seconds.

Developments in *Mitteleuropa*

HUNGARY'S CHANGING position as a state and political entity was paradoxical in the period of 1914 to 1950, when it moved psychologically from middle – or *Mitteleuropa* – to eastern Europe, from a junior partner in the chaotic, ethnically diverse Austro-Hungarian Empire to virtual vassal status under the USSR by 1950. In 1914 Budapest was, along with Vienna and Prague, one of the intellectual and artistic centres of Europe. Enzo Traverso in 2016's *Fire and Blood: The European Civil War* stressed that there were and still are different interpretations of the concept of *Mitteleuropa*, and one was identified as the legacy of the vast multinational and cosmopolitan Habsburg Empire. It was here in the first decades of the 20th century that the genius of Freud, Einstein, Kafka and Klimt flourished.

The central European position acted as a crossroads of Germanic, Slavic and Latin cultures and a mixture of religions – Protestant, Catholic, Orthodox and, to a lesser extent, Muslim. Hungary as a separate state was forged after World War One when the treaties of the victors broke up the Austro-Hungarian Empire into new smaller multi-states with all the confusion, pain and anger that such a process brings. This state of affairs existed during the tensions of the interwar period and, after the annihilating destruction of World War Two, Hungary entered another period from small central European state to a component of the USSR's land-based empire with state socialist structures imposed from Moscow and the ever-present, occupying Red Army, which radically altered the descriptive of Europe to a dichotomy of east and west even if Budapest is indisputably located in central Europe.

World War Two had catastrophic effects on vast spaces of the European continent and Hungary was no exception. The Hungarian economy was devastated with infrastructure critically fractured, which was only compounded in the mid-to-late 1940s by the Soviet removal of vast amounts of machinery and raw materials and the undoubted burden of quartering hundreds of thousands of Soviet troops. These harsh terms led to an increase in national inflation, to the highest rate ever recorded. In the summer of 1946 the inflation rate was rising at around 10 per cent to 12 per cent per hour and resulted in bank notes with near endless zeroes on them, with values not just in the billions but the trillions and even quadrillions. Fundamentally cash, at this time in Hungary, became worthless.

The response of the USSR to this economic and financial meltdown was to instigate a hardline Stalinist structure, under Mátyás Rákosi, who led Hungary between 1949 and 1953. Known as 'Stalin's best pupil' with all the chilling reality that moniker inferred, Rákosi and his apparatchiks brought their own terror with mass charges of individual offences against the state and around 200,000 suffering forced labour, internment and imprisonment. Straight-out execution of political opponents and criminals was common during this period, as was death via torture from the state security authority, the AVH. And 1953 was a key year for Hungary's state socialist political machine due to the death of Joseph Stalin in March of that year. The exceedingly harsh regime run under the auspices of Stalinist diktat, with its focussed approach to the development of heavy industry, had led to resentment, anger and deep discontent in the majority of the population with material privation, cultural monotheism and genuine fear of the AVH. Upon Stalin's death and the subsequent denouncement of him in Nikita Khrushchev's supposedly secret speech to the Congress of the Communist Party of the Soviet Union in February 1956, there was a shift away from the worst excesses of the leadership of the likes of Rákosi. He was accused of the crime of developing a cult of personality and removing the collective leadership to that of an individual. What followed in this post-Stalinist approach and the toppling of Rákosi was known as the New Course. The New Course brought a level of relief from the worst terrors of Stalinism and the Hungarian people would not easily submit to any external reimposition of such abusive structures.

Through all this pain and suffering for the Hungarian people and their domination by others there was one area where the ordinary person could take pride and joy, from their national football team, their results and from a player so special he will forever occupy one of the very highest levels on Mount Olympus – Ferenc Puskás. The Hungarian Communist regime saw football as a useful propaganda tool because as a team sport it exemplified the positive aspects of communism – teamwork aiming at a specific goal with all individuals fulfilling their role for the greater good. Overall Hungary went 13 years without a home defeat, from losing 7-2 to Sweden in 1943 to Czechoslovakia beating them 4-2 in 1956. For the golden period of the Golden Team the list of results was incredible and though England's humiliating defeats were very important for both sides they were partly just two results among many spectacular scorelines for the *Aranycsapat* between 1947 and the 1954 World Cup. The cascade of goals over the seven-year period was led by Puskás and Sándor Kocsis, who scored 158 international goals between them in one of the most potent striking partnerships in the history of the game. Between 1947 and 1954 Hungary racked up at least a six-goal total in one game every year. Some of the results bordered on schoolboy level as they stretched their long unbeaten run.

If anyone at the FA or the English press had been interested in obtaining a record of results, they may have anticipated that Hungary would almost certainly score a considerable number of goals in their two internationals against England in London and Budapest. All the information was there for anyone to see that this would have been true to form for the incredible attacking options of the Magyars. They started off their high scoring run with a 9-0 home demolition of Bulgaria in August 1947. In 1948 alone Hungary put seven past Switzerland, destroyed Romania 9-0 and then scored six away in Poland. The high scoring continued unabated in 1949 with six against Austria, eight versus Poland and then 5-0 in consecutive games at home to Bulgaria and Sweden. There was no let-up in the juggernaut in 1950 as they secured their third 5-0 win on the run against Czechoslovakia and then in September destroyed poor old Albania 12-0. In 1951 Poland were once again totally dispatched, this time 6-0 in May and Finland 8-0 in November and in a follow-up international in June 1952 Finland were again swatted aside 6-1. During the Hungarians' Olympics triumph, also in Finland, a month later they trounced Turkey 7-1 and then just four days later it was Sweden's turn to taste a 6-0 defeat, later in the year Czechoslovakia were dispatched 5-0 at home.

You almost need to take a breath reading through the list of non-stop spectacular results over those six years. Did any international team ever have a run like that? Not just a question of a long unbeaten sequence but destruction after destruction, racking up five and six in every other fixture. This was the team and the record that, according to Willy Meisl, 90 per cent of the English press thought England were going to uphold their unbeaten record at home to. The problem was always going to be defensive and dealing with the conundrum of trying to stop a team that scored so many goals. Of course, there are extra questions with this data – Winterbottom and Rous would have access to this list of results, but did the press? Certainly, the Olympics were high-profile and newsworthy but how many English journalists were interested in or could find out about Hungarian victories over the likes of Albania or Finland?

Though there may have been some difficulty in finding out specific match results there were two areas of Hungary's approach to football that were newsworthy before the 6-3 game. One was the inclusiveness of their training techniques and the other was the special player and person that was Ferenc Puskás. Puskás was the player allowed to function differently for Hungary due to his exceptional talent, and like Garrincha and Maradona he was beloved by the people not just for his amazing skill level but because of his personality. When FIFA wanted to dedicate the award for the best goal scored in world football each year they chose Puskás. The greatest goal in the world every year is named after the king of the *Aranycsapat*. The fantasy level of these goals was irreparably linked with a fantasy player of the highest possible level. Puskás held the divide, he was a player of the ultimate echelon, but he had the connection with the people he came from. He forever retained his image as a bit of a scallywag with a naughty twinkle in his eye and a solid confidence that often exudes from those with a special gift.

In England, Puskás's main nickname was the 'Galloping Major' as a comment on him technically being in the Hungarian army and the Honvéd team, but this was a bizarre misnomer on two counts – he wasn't a major and he didn't gallop. The nickname he was known by in Hungary, throughout his life and with deep affection was 'Ocsi', meaning little brother. He was my little brother, your little brother and, more importantly, the nation's little brother, forever connecting Puskás as part of the Hungarian people, as part of your family. This innate connection gave Puskás an overwhelming confidence in himself as a person, based around his special skills. Puskás knew his value to Hungary and the communist state and sports ministry and as the supreme player of the Golden Team. When Puskás was once challenged by party servants about his lifestyle and fundamental political neutrality he was quick to respond that they could be found behind any desk whereas there was only one Puskás.

Perhaps the most fantastical element in the whole pattern of play of the Hungarian team was the non-coached relationship between the two core players – Puskás and József Bozsik. The connection was beyond coaching as it developed at the absolute ground zero of childhood friendship. Incredibly, Puskás and Bozsik grew up as neighbours in the same building. According to Gyorgy Szollosi in *Puskás*, they grew up side-by-side with interconnected families and walked to school together.

The two friends engaged in thousands of hours of pure football together – street football. Their skills were developed not in isolation until honed by Béla Guttmann at Honvéd but enhanced together in harmony. The timing of the run and the through pass had been shared 10,000 times before playing for Honvéd or the national team together. Bozsik controlled the midfield and fuelled Puskás's forward penetration and his 84 goals in 85 internationals. Despite all the written commentary on the levels of coaching and teamwork preparation no system could penetrate that depth of relationship and connectivity. England picked players in the 6-3 match who had never lined up with the person next to them before and never would again. Hungary picked at the core of their team two men who as kids had a special knock on the wall connecting their flats to communicate going out to play football together.

Hungary didn't beat England 6-3 in November 1953 necessarily because they had better players in every position, but because they were a unit developed over time at just two clubs – Jenő Buzánszky at right-back was the only member of the national team who didn't play for either Honvéd or MTK. Puskás played for the army team, the renamed Honvéd, from the smaller more local club Kispest, where one of the coaches, the peripatetic Béla Guttmann, was ensconced from 1948. Honvéd were one of a collection of teams in communist Europe to be theoretical representatives of the army, joining Legia in Warsaw, Partizan in Belgrade, Dukla in Prague and CSKA in both Sofia and Moscow. The name Honvéd, meaning 'Defender of the Motherland', dated from the 1848 Magyar revolt with the Holy Roman Empire against the Austrians. Unsurprisingly, as the army used classic carrot and stick techniques, the best youth players elected to play for Honvéd and to join Puskás in the all-powerful unit which doubled as the core of the national team.

Clearly the regularity of playing and training together as a unit increased understanding and communication to a level required for the 'whirl' approach to succeed effectively. The interchange of positions and fluid movement of players in attack mode could only function correctly through practice and training as a unit together. Nothing in football looks more ridiculous than the pass into empty space harmlessly slipping out of play or safely into the goalkeeper's hands, due to miscommunication between passer and receiver.

In contemporary comment Brian Glanville in *Soccer Nemesis* concluded that Puskás was so devastating because he combined the artistry and craft of the older schools of football with the power and speed of modern play. Puskás was by Glanville's argument an axiomatic modern player. Puskás never appeared to be a party man such as Bozsik, nor was he openly antagonistic to the Communist Party hierarchy like Grosics. He was a canny individual who lived in a country run by an oppressive regime. He was an extremely popular man who utilised his fame and privileged position for his own ends. The achievements of top-level sportsmen and women were connected to the heroic role of 'the people'. Puskás as team captain was the face of the *Aranycsapat* and regularly appeared on state-controlled newsreels promising future glories on the football pitch and accepting praise and congratulations from the people for their 'unforgettable achievement' of the 6-3 victory. In the international press Puskás was a canny operator too, offering opinion but tailoring it to the readership. In an interview with *World Sports Magazine,* he was clear that though England's soccer supremacy of old was over, the lessons from Hungary's two victories had been learned and England were on their way back to the top, predicting a win for them in an upcoming international against the defending world champions West Germany in late 1954.

Puskás himself concluded that it was not specifically the positioning of Hidegkuti which was the devastating factor in the 6-3 victory. The most important factor was the gap in preparation between England and Hungary. As quoted by Glanville again in *Wembley 1923–1973: The Official Wembley Story of Fifty Years*, Puskás was deeply critical of the unpreparedness of the English defence for the method of attack adopted by himself and fellow Hungarian forwards. England were not prepared for the situations developed by Hungary and therefore couldn't cope, particularly with the concept that attacks were led from behind or what Willy Meisl called Puskás's 'ice hockey' passes near goal. In an article entitled 'The Welcome Invaders' in *World Sports Magazine*, Meisl referred to the hard, accurate passing of the ball, which helped a player into a promising position.

Another interested and thoughtful observer of Puskás's play was former top professional turned journalist and commentator Charles Buchan. In his own magazine, *Charles Buchan's Football Monthly*, he was an unequivocal admirer of Puskás and drew particular attention to the strengths of his positional sense and strong use of the short pass, while showing clever movement when in possession. England's major issue, as Puskás interpreted it, was that they were not a team at all but 11 individuals. He saw them as more of a unit in that 1954 interview than previously and encouraged a 'new reform plan' to be initiated with a focus on bringing a body of the players together more often. This was a key factor for Puskás in England's future development, 'In a really well-trained ensemble every player must know his partners thoroughly and sense in advance where his colleagues will send the ball.'

An article reported Puskás's views in a respectful and slightly ingratiating manner then tumbled over into fantasy when Puskás stated, 'At Wembley, England gave Hungary a very good game ... if our team had not been in particularly good form we would have been held to a draw.' Apart from this bit of playing to the crowd Puskás offered some clear, solid advice for what England needed to do to bolster their game – alter the predictability of play, 'block' pick players for the national team from two or three club sides, as was the pattern in Hungary, and a more thoughtful cultivation of youth and English league clubs could copy continental playing styles. Walter Winterbottom may well have read this article and quietly agreed with some of these points that Puskás raised, particularly altering play and an effective youth programme.

In the tumult of Hungarian politics in the mid-1950s the Golden Team became *personae non gratae* after 1956 with the new communist regime established from Moscow, particularly after Puskás, Kocsis and Zoltán Czibor all went into exile. Only three years earlier the team had been the centre of rapturous celebration with hundreds of people sending in poems to the editor of *Nepsport* in honour of the 6-3 victory. After 1956, according to Gyorgy Szollosi in *Puskás*, it wasn't until 40 years later at Christmas 1996 that there was a sense of full rehabilitation, when half the country sat down for a television special where the whole 6-3 match was shown for the first time on Hungarian television. This was followed later by Puskás's own personal rehabilitation when the UEFA Congress posthumously awarded him the Order of Merit in Emerald, the highest possible. From the late 1970s onwards, author Tony Pawson held the view that Puskás was the only player to really rival Pelé, and even when he looked overweight and unathletic later in his career at Real Madrid he never lost his swift acceleration, the certainty of finishing with that lethal left foot and shots from unexpected angles and distances. Of course, this statement was made pre-Diego Maradona, Zinedine Zidane, Lionel Messi and Cristiano Ronaldo, but by 1978 there had been Johan Cruyff,

Eusébio, Alfredo Di Stéfano and Gerd Müller. Perhaps Pawson was right, in the sense that you can't really argue with 84 goals in 85 international matches.

Puskás was, for all his natural talent, partially a product of training. The training and development of players in Hungary began with junior and youth programmes. The junior game was built on a lighter ball and smaller pitch with an initial programme of physical education being devised by MTK under a true socialist motto of 'Ready for work and fight', taught by qualified trainers. The next phase was the introduction of tactics based on teamwork and the teaching of positional play. Coaches kept training diaries on individual players and specific training programmes were developed from this. All this was at youth level, in advance of most, if not all, professional clubs' routines in England.

A major resource subsequently utilised by young players was *Learn to Play the Hungarian Way* published by the Hungarian Sports Publishing House. With a subtitle of 'A Soccer Manual for Young Footballers, Showing the Methods Used by the Hungarian Champions', there was no doubting its message. It was co-written by Jenő Csaknády, a leading Hungarian expert in gymnastics and physical culture, and Márton Bukovi, who was a former Hungarian international and master of technique. The basis for all their tutoring was that the game was based on the three Bs – Brains, Ball Control and Body Balance. All technical skill and tactical awareness grew from this base. The training manual covered a broad range of skills development including shooting, heading and trapping the ball. It then moved on to more advanced areas such as developing boundary vision and tactical systems. These developments and programmes by the Hungarians were what awaited the English national team on 25 November 1953.

PART TWO: DURING

25 November 1953

THE DREARY day of 25 November 1953 finally arrived, when any one of the vast Wembley crowd could have spent a few minutes thinking about how they were living Thomas Hood's poem *November*. The other option was to ignore the dank and misty atmosphere and lose themselves in the match programme.

The document clearly showed a split that existed in 1953 between those who were knowledgeable about international football developments and those who were overwhelmingly British-centric. The rather slim programme, fortunately not bloated with seemingly endless pages of adverts, sponsorship deals and merchandise, gave a clear insight into 1953 England and more specifically football within the country at that time. On page five, in a brief article by John Graydon, was all anyone needed to know in a nutshell about the Hungarians and their play: 'Olympic champions, famous the world over for their beautiful football, and ranked by every authority as the finest side in Europe, Hungary are assured of a warm welcome by everyone at Wembley, for few teams have come to the home of association football with a bigger or more just reputation.' Graydon concluded, 'They are the best continental team I have ever seen.' So all any of the players that day had to do was turn to this piece and the task in hand would all have been made perfectly clear.

On the front cover of the programme was the semi-roofed Wembley, still called the Empire Stadium after its original construction for the Empire Exhibition of 1924, and the Union flag by the side of England, denoting the interchangeability between England and Britain. In the display of flags this lasted well into the 1990s when England fans claimed the cross of St George as English, rather than the Union flag. This was decades after Scottish and Welsh fans had shown a more public allegiance to the Saltire and the Welsh dragon.

The Hungarian team's warm-up caused gasps and head-shaking among many watching England fans, but they were, no doubt, comforted by the 65 minutes of marching band music from the central band of the RAF playing a special selection of items including 'Bond of Friendship' and a piece called 'Hungaria', which was referred to as a fantasia.

The overall tone of the programme was set immediately in the welcome page with a piece enthusing about Hungary and their strong world reputation, which was then dutifully translated into Magyar below. The key article in the programme was another piece by Graydon entitled 'Hungary's Olympic Winners are Welcome'. This was a deep and penetrating article eulogising over all aspects of the Hungarian team and their play. It made clear for any England fan walking up Wembley Way who may have thought their team would win comfortably that this was not going to happen.

Graydon assessed Hungary as players of beautiful football, ranked the finest side in Europe, who were class and masters of a football with distribution a lesson to others, as was their sportsmanship. Despite the wholly positive descriptions, Graydon, who watched Hungary in their recent international against Sweden, made his most interesting points in areas not frequently covered by other commentators. He turned his focus to other developments that affected him when he visited Hungary – he was deeply impressed by the superman level of physical fitness of the *Aranycsapat* and how this had been achieved by a combination of cross-country runs and gymnastics, which was an area of training Billy Wright wanted to see more of a focus on. Other areas that clearly stood out for Graydon and that he wished to inform the Wembley attendees of were the desire that the Hungarians had to learn of the English game and that the football structure was already focussing on the next generation of stars with a comprehensive programme on youth players with regular coaching input from star players such as Puskás and Grosics.

In contrast to this knowledge and appreciation of Hungary was the line-up positioning printed in the centre pages, following the standard format of both sides fielding a 2-3-5 formation with five forwards spread across the pitch. England's Matthews, Taylor, Mortensen, Sewell and Finney (replaced by Robb) were matched by Czibor, Puskás, Hidegkuti, Kocsis and Budai. The core issue for England, of course, was that Hungary did not play in this designated formation. Almost all of the England support crammed into Wembley had never seen Hungary and their system before – they'd never seen the 'whirl' in the central field or the described 'withdrawn number ten' role of Hidegkuti, who was numbered nine and listed at centre-forward in the programme. It's no wonder most of the 100,000 crowd were amazed by Hungary's play and positioning as the programme they bought bore little resemblance to what happened on the pitch in front of them.

Kit

SUCH IS the iconic nature of how the 6-3 match has been viewed that even comments on areas such as kit, the pre-match preparation and the walk on to the pitch are all maintained as contrasting absolutes. In reality the position and awareness of, say, kit was more complex than the clear dichotomy repeatedly presented. Incredibly, as recounted by Tom Finney, in the 1950s the England team were provided with just one shirt size for all players. Regardless of whether you were small and slight like Matthews or a strapping centre-forward, the one size was deemed acceptable – whether it strangled you or made you look like a child wearing adult clothes.

The most contrasting element of kit was, unquestionably, boots. Billy Wright's oft-recorded comment about the Hungarian boots was, 'We should be all right today lads, they [Hungary] haven't even brought the right kit.' In the web of myth-making its not even clear whether he did actually say this. What is amazing about this statement is that Wright was fundamentally positioning the Hungarians as being all aspects of the unknown. Hungary's shirts were more tailored and tight fitting, expanding Puskás's tummy; their shorts were shorter and lighter, and their boots were certainly more modern in their shape and styling. This type of kit was basically unknown in the English Football League, but it was not unknown or unseen to the smaller number of England players who played, in a limited sense, on a world stage. This tag applies to no one more than Wright himself. In the 1950 World Cup the England players had certainly seen lightweight boots. Stanley Matthews was so intrigued by the little carpet slippers he'd seen in Brazil that he bought several pairs to take back to England with him. He reputedly had a cobbler in Stoke-on-Trent who made him endless new pairs as they only lasted for two or three games. Matthews was no fool and he was obsessive about his own performance. He realised immediately what these slimline, lighter boots could give him – an advantage.

The kit and boots were not an unknown to a cohort of players on the field – Wright, Matthews, Ramsey, Mortensen and Dickinson, or Finney in the press box. As well as in Brazil, they had also experienced it during their recent summer tour of South America. The 1953 trip was England's first to Latin America, playing Argentina, Uruguay and Chile and finishing up in New York against the USA. The Latin American football nations had been wearing the more modern-style kit and boots for numerous years. There was experience of viewing this lighter kit before the 6-3 game but even this fundamental was not changed after it. The more decisive change came several months later, following the 1954 Switzerland World Cup. The heavier, older-style shirts, with a button or lace at the top, were phased out for the slip-on tops. Norman Giller's biography of Billy Wright stated that the older, heavier kit and boots were removed from the England scene with almost immediate effect after the 6-3 defeat. This was a recommendation of Football League managers who were consulted by the FA in the aftermath. However, this simply wasn't the case and as with so many aspects of responses to England's defeat it was an evolutionary change after the 1954 World Cup rather than a fast-paced revolutionary process.

The England shirts resembled those that working men wore in a range of manual jobs, and the football boots resembled the toughest work boots just with studs nailed into them. All English boots from the early 1950s focussed on power – the Hotshot or the Mansfield Hotspur are prime examples with their reinforced toecaps and at least two inches of protective leather over the ankle. Work boots built for going to work in, for power, clattering and battering, built to last through the English season with pitches in every possible condition from rock solid to a slithering, muddy swamp.

One of the main advertising avenues for the boot companies was the *Official FA Yearbook*, an annual with a wide range of articles and tactical diagrams. The edition for 1954/55 season alone had multiple adverts for the old-style high boot – the Arthur Rowe Streamline, West Bromwich Albion's choice for the FA Cup Final, or the Hotshot Association Football boot made by Wellingborough Boot and Shoe Manufacturer. All of these boots advertised in this premier annual, no doubt charging considerable advertising rates, were for the high, full boot, not the more modern shoe. The atmosphere and reality of English football after the 6-3 was an evolution not a revolution in changes to kit as much as any other aspect of the game.

The shorts hadn't really changed for 20 years or more. A more accurate word would be 'middles' as two pairs of shorts could easily be made from one pair of classic middles. Altering the regular look of classic British shorts could be dangerous to the image of British manhood. At the FA Cup Final in May 1953, Bolton Wanderers had unveiled and worn lighter shorts with a satin finish and a stripe down the side. During the formal introduction before the match an air of embarrassment was palpable, Only for the players' concerns to be confirmed by the Duke of Edinburgh, who informed them they 'looked like a bunch of pansies'.

One of the leading football writers of the 1950s, Geoffrey Green, wrote in his 1974 book *Soccer in the Fifties* about the changes to kit in England that were introduced over the course of that decade. He also cited the turning point in this development as the 1954 World Cup, not the Hungary matches. Hungary were just one of the multiple teams in Switzerland who had long eschewed kit which made, in Green's words, the England team look as incongruous as pre-First World War female tennis players with their long, full skirts to the modern 1970s eye. Green rather obliquely connected changes in football shirts and shorts to reduction on British conservatism and the 'explosion' in youth culture.

However, Green did have a more grounded comment to make on the progress of boots in England in the 1950s. This was a 'dramatic' development with the arrival of the 'ballet' type of boot. In contrast to comments by Wright and others of the Hungarians' appearance, Green informed us that this style of boot was first seen at the Wembley international against Austria in 1951 and that in this match some of the boots were dyed red or blue. The detractors were concerned that though these slimline boots made control better, what they termed as 'ballet boots' would not last in English weather conditions of rain, mud, snow and ice. Clearly none of these detractors had been to Austria in January.

Merrick, Ramsey, Eckersley, Wright and Dickinson all played in the Austria game, so the view presented that the Hungary kit was a completely new and alien experience is not a particularly truthful one. Green, for one, was pleased to see the back of the old-style full boots that he described as 'monstrous heavyweights fit only for infantrymen fighting in the mud of Flanders'. Shin pads changed too, to a smaller and lighter design, as the old boots were phased out, the tackling was not so heavy and the older-style shinguards were not required.

Green saw the introduction of the new, lighter kit as a clear physical embodiment of British football beginning to adopt a continental method. The long-established outlook of a hard-tackling and demonstrably physical approach was the style retained in England, but the other countries imposed their specific national characteristics on the game. Green saw these as 'ballet' and of 'intellectual ball play'. The coffee house tactics and the style of *Mitteleuropa* come to mind.

Green was presenting a double insult in his vocabulary, connecting the move to modern kit as the two prongs of a concerning development – effeminate and intellectual, both attributes had no place in British football. The creators of the game who'd held strong in their isolationist approach for 90 years, according to Green, were now not just taking up new outlooks and ideas as manifested in kit changes but had 'begun to follow in the footsteps of others'.

Warm-up and Pre-match Routine

THE DIFFERENCES continued before the match began. Very few fixtures can ever have had the warm-up and pre-match routine so assiduously commented on, both at the time and reinforced over a period of more than 60 years. The novelty for England fans was that there actually was a warm-up as English teams didn't usually participate in such a routine; they just walked out on to the pitch five minutes before kick-off. The Hungarians were different in many ways, including how they shared their skill before the match had even begun. One of the many individuals who shaped English club football in the next 30 years was Malcolm Allison, who was in the crowd that day. He, for one, was impressed both by the concept of a warm-up and the fact that two players 'volleyed the ball to each other eight times over a 25-yard distance without it touching the ground'. The Hungarians were making their statement to the crowd and observers. Tom Finney, in the press box, had a similar conclusion to Allison of admiration. There was, however, general confusion among the British journalists as to why Hungary were on the pitch 20 minutes before kick-off and what the purpose of their set routines was.

The confidence of showing skills moved to captain Ferenc Puskás a few seconds before kick-off. Perhaps a ball-juggling sequence of jaw-dropping proportions has been lost from the film we can see today but the skills routine Puskás went through was of a no more sensational level than any modern semi-professional player would comfortably achieve. Was Puskás just killing a few seconds in the centre circle before kick-off or was the mischievous one nonchalantly showing off the pure skills of a footballing genius honed on the streets of Budapest? Personally, I'd choose the latter, as what was incredible about this 20-second display of skill was the impact it had on those watching. His opposing captain Billy Wright was in awe, as was commentator Kenneth Wolstenholme, who said on the coverage that he had never seen anything like it. Harry Johnston was far more phlegmatic about the whole skills debate, as he stated in *Rocky Road to Wembley* that the only reason Puskás's display worked was because no one had ever seen something like that before, and then after that extraordinary statement he returned to the oft-repeated comment that how would these tricks fare on the heavy, muddy English league pitches.

During the walk-out and pre-match routine players and observers got their glimpse of a further example of controversy – Puskás's tummy. There is probably no other point or representation that epitomises the mixed memories and mixed reporting of the 6-3 game than the dimensions of Ferenc's middle region. Just how big was it in November 1953? This assessment and comment confirm the absolute confusion of who knew what and who said what from the England team and commentators. No one ever described Puskás as svelte or having the body of a Greek Adonis and he was, by his own admission, clearly a man who loved his food. In the latter 1950s after several months of inactivity when he signed for Real Madrid there's no question that

Alfredo Di Stefano's cutting put-down to Puskás of 'panzon' was an accurate one. However, in 1953 it wasn't so clear-cut. In a famous side-on photo of Hungary in line-up before the 6-3 game Puskás has, to quote Allison 'a little tummy on him', but the subsequent comments from the England players of how they perceived Puskás in the tunnel and the walk on to the pitch were far more negative. Hungary's shirts were modern with a tailored fit, rather than England's smock affair, so any tummy bulge would be more obvious. The novelty of this type of kit was overplayed by some of the England team and so was the size of Puskás's stomach. In a memory established after the game it ever expanded and was a constant point of comment down the decades.

Passage of Play

AFTER THE otherness of the kit, the warm-up, the pre-match and the differing views of Puskás's belly it was time for the true otherness to reveal itself. One minute was all it took for the new reality to begin shaping itself. The new order was set immediately from the kick-off as space and movement dominated. Hidegkuti's powerful angled shot smashed into the net as if driven by Thor's hammer, but the important component was really the space he found for himself and the time he was allowed to shoot. In the Pathé News highlight reel, confusion reigned early as Wolstenholme filled his commentary with oohs and aahs. He explained early on to the watching England fans in the darkened seats in the cinemas of Norwich and Newcastle that the Hungarian number five was not the centre-half and that the outside-left Czibor was now on the right wing. Wolstenholme made an interesting comment about Puskás when saying, 'We ought to have Puskás on the music hall with his tricks.' The comment would be interpreted in a negative context other than being plain appreciation of Puskás's skill level. Perhaps Wolstenholme was stressing that there was no place for such trickery on the serious arena of a football pitch for an international match.

Watching at 70 years removed, the first thing that strikes you is the reduced speed of the game and the time that the players have on the ball. From 1953 to 2023 football, certainly in England, has got inexorably faster and faster. It's difficult to even notice or quantify, like the glacial change in language, when watching games on a weekly basis. It's only when we remove ourselves and look at a game from so far back in time that all those incremental changes accumulate to conclude a chasm from 1953 to now. Hungary were, without question, a technical team but the time they were allowed on the ball, for a player to move into space and the pass selected, made it so easy coming forward. From the footage that survives one overriding factor that is not usually covered is the number of times the England players needlessly lost possession. It was endless. For all the praise heaped on the Hungarian team down the decades and their 'new' system of play, England made it so easy for Hungary as they constantly lost possession due to poor touches and inaccurate passing and let Hungary move forward with another flowing move.

After the first rocket shot in minute one, Hungary had their first phase of near total domination where they created multiple chances from their off-the-ball movement and accurate passing but didn't quickly extend their lead. There were options and chances galore in the first ten to 15 minutes, but the score remained 1-0. It should have been 2-0 when a perfectly good goal by Hidegkuti was ruled offside. England survived these early sequences of build-up play and against this tidal wave they scored an equaliser with a goal of power and pace through the middle, culminating in a nice, angled shot by Sewell. Despite this setback and clear frustration from Hungarian defenders at conceding, the Magyars stuck to their style of play and coach Sebes's thoroughly crafted plan to initiate perhaps the most devastating period of play from visiting opponents at Wembley, up to this point.

The next 15 minutes saw the score go to 2-1 then 3-1 then 4-1. Hungary regained the lead five minutes after Sewell's equaliser in a rather mundane manner with Hidegkuti stabbing one in from close range. Then they moved on to another level of fantasy football, culminating in the most famous goal of the game, Puskás's drag-back finish. No doubt it was a skill attempted in thousands of school playgrounds in the following weeks. After Billy Wright had pulled the grass out of his mouth and Gil Merrick, who was a statue as Puskás's shot flew past him from a few feet, picked the ball out of the net, Hungary inflicted further humiliation on England with a deflected goal from Puskás.

Trailing 4-1 in under 30 minutes, England desperately needed some form of positive response. Anything was required to stop the seemingly endless flow of Hungarian attacks. England never stopped trying and for a brief period up to half-time they, at least, were competing on the same level as Hungary. There was not the fluid approach of the visitors but there was energy and high tempo as Stan Mortensen pulled one back and George Robb had a strong header denied by Grosics. Wright saw that specific save as crucial in the passage of the game and scoreline. Maybe if Robb's header had gone in to make it 4-3 then things might possibly have been different, but as the Dutch say, 'If my aunt had balls, she'd be my uncle.'

Grosics made a somewhat theatrical Hollywood save and that was that. What had looked like desperate annihilation after Puskás scored the Hungarian fourth within half an hour was at least held to four up to half-time. England continued to push back the onslaught at the start of the second half with attempts from Mortensen. However, the pattern of the game moved back to Hungary nine minutes after half-time when after considerable ping-pong action, a strong long-range shot from Bozsik flew home. This was the one effort from distance that Merrick probably should have done better with. Hungary scored their sixth and final goal two minutes later with a flowing team move involving over half of their players and finished off by Hidegkuti for his international hat-trick at Wembley, still a very rare achievement.

Six Hungarian goals in 60 minutes and none thereafter. How common a happening this is when one team has dominated and is so comfortably in the lead, then the level and intensity drop. As the first half of Germany v Brazil in the 2014 World Cup semi-final was sensational at 5-0 to Germany, so was the second half a pedestrian non-event at Wembley. Hungary had come to London with a well-prepared side and executed their plan to overwhelm and destroy England, which they achieved in 56 minutes. The only further score was England's third five minutes later when Ramsey, as calm as always, hit a low drive past Grosics for his second penalty in two international matches. Thirty minutes later his England career ended. After they had conceded the sixth goal, the dejection of the England players was palpable in their body language as they walked back to the centre circle – without doubt any professional player in a team who had let in six goals with 30 minutes to play must have been contemplating how many would be conceded at the end of play. Perhaps some were already thinking about who was to blame, who made the crucial mistakes? Ramsey was quick to lay the responsibility on goalkeeper Merrick, particularly the three long-range shots that resulted in goals.

In 2003 the BBC produced a commemorative piece celebrating 50 years since the 6-3 match. This consisted mostly of Bobby Robson and stalwart commentator John

Motson watching clips of the game. Even so far on and after the thousands of games Robson was involved in as a player, manager and observer all over the world, he still held a view of being in awe of Hungary. 'Men from Mars,' he described them as, and in a sweeping analysis he was convinced the Magical Magyars 'kiboshed the WM system in 90 minutes' and moved English teams into playing 4-2-4. Interestingly, it was the movement of players that most impressed the young Robson watching from the stands. Once again this was a process of evolution not revolution. Robson was clear to stress to Motson and the viewers that it was Winterbottom who brought in 4-2-4 to his coaching courses and that the importance of Winterbottom in the development of English football was through his role as director of coaching.

Robson also argued that the 6-3 game was a categorical catalyst in changing football thinking in England and a specific example of this was the increase in training with the ball from the 1954/55 season onwards, perhaps suggesting that this nine-month delay could be put down more to the cumulative effect of the two Hungary defeats and the 1954 World Cup and the level of performance from other teams such as Brazil and Uruguay. In an earlier interview with Billy Wright, long retired at that point, the former captain claimed to the camera that he and the England players in general had no previous knowledge of Hidegkuti and his withdrawn position behind Puskás and Kocsis.

In addition to the whole 90 minutes being available, there are highlights reels which present the match in a condensed presentation of five to seven minutes. This helps form a different match interpretation so familiar to football fans in formats such as *Match of the Day*, but in the 1950s the footage was provided by such services as Pathé News and British Movietone News. Pathé News's presentation stated that at a full Wembley the visitors were recognised as the best side in Europe and were complimented for their teamwork. In contrast England were categorised through the abilities of individuals – Matthews was the maestro and the wizard, with Mortensen as a human dynamo. Even in this short, seven-minute piece which covered nine goals, it was apparent how rigid England were and they appeared to be a disorganised group of men who just happened to be on a football pitch together. This slowness and apparent disorganisation presented Hungary with a lot of time and space to weave their patterns.

At the end of the match, as the England players traipsed off looking dejected, Hungary were confirmed by the commentator as the most brilliant team whose performance was enough to 'shatter' England's unbeaten home record. In the effusive conclusions we moved into the realms of fantasy, stating the Magyars had an 'iron curtain' defence, which was absolutely not the case having conceded three goals. Hungary's strength was most definitely not as a defensive unit. No doubt the commentator had been desperate to shoehorn in this zeitgeist geopolitical comment at some point.

For Movietone it was Leslie Mitchell reporting in the beautiful, clipped tones later parodied by following generations as the perfect BBC voice. Mitchell reconfirmed exoticism of the opponents by stating, 'The scorer's name is pronounced Hidegkuti, I hope.' The small coterie of Hungary fans were shown enthusiastically supporting their team and rather hilariously there were shots of the Hungarian substitutes watching the match from behind the goal, sat on footballs and smoking cigarettes. Though Sebes initiated his revolutionary tactics on the pitch, clearly smoking cessation for his players was not so high on the agenda, or perhaps that was why the substitutes were all the way over behind the goals so that Sebes couldn't quite see them through the mist. Mitchell also went high in the effusiveness stakes, concluding that Hungary had completed an 'absolute orgy of scoring'.

The Players and Management

Gil Merrick: the Self-Perceived Visionary

In his wonderfully titled autobiography from 1954, *I See it All*, Gilbert Merrick espoused at length on the incredible game against Hungary where he conceded seven in Budapest. Paradoxically and strangely, the 6-3 defeat was barely mentioned. Clearly the 7-1 debacle had had a level of psychological effect on Merrick, but his observations and assessment of the Hungarian and English game had more depth and sophistication than many of the other players from the 6-3 defeat. Harry Johnston and Alf Ramsey's views were pure jingoism while Stanley Matthews's answer was simply to return to England's strengths that had worked in the past, but not really outlining what those strengths were.

Merrick was nothing if not open and honest in his approach. His focus was the gap between Hungary and England in almost all areas of the pitch. About the Budapest match, Merrick openly admitted that his overriding concern was just how many goals England were going to concede. At 6-0 down with a quarter of the match remaining he appeared deeply focussed on the gigantic catastrophe enveloping the team. Merrick identified several consistent factors which gave the Hungarians their dominance – speed, accurate passes, possession-based play, control of the game through ball retention, individual ball skills and techniques the

Hungarians developed in abundance which were, according to Merrick, missing from the English game.

In a beautiful piece of self-defence Merrick stated that it was only down to him that Hungary's final goal tally stayed under ten. Seven goals scored by 72 minutes on the clock and Hungary had three clear-cut chances to make the score even more devastating, but for Merrick saving from József Tóth and Puskás twice. This is the first example of a consistent theme of those who played for England in the two Hungary matches of a considerable absence of personal responsibility for their part in these annihilations. Merrick's position can be summarised thus – the team, overall, were lacking in almost all areas but fundamentally it was mostly other areas of the team that were to blame, and I did my best.

Merrick stressed two main options in how to deal with Hungarian play – to pack the defence, as Sweden did in a 2-2 draw just before the 6-3 match, or to develop a high-powered attack which would go for goals. Basically, Merrick reduced football to ultra-defence or ultra-attack. His vague concept for ultra-attack must have appeared more appealing to England fans in 1954, with professional football returning to its roots of near pure attack, football of the school playground from Blackburn to Bogotá. Merrick foresaw the future of football as a list of results of 8-7, 9-8 or even 10-9. Ironically, he couldn't have been more wrong as to how football at the higher echelons would develop into the 1960s with the widespread success of the Italian *catenaccio* approach and the perfection of the 1-0 result. One could imagine in the early 1960s Helenio Herrera relaxing in a little Italian café, calmly sipping his espresso while flicking through *I See it All* and his eyes resting on these recommendations on page 93. No doubt he would have almost choked to death on a delicate pastry at the thought of a professional match ending at 7-6 or heaven forbid 10-9.

Merrick's recommendations were made in a period where he seemed to be generally uncertain about Hungarian play and how to respond, but at least he was responding and thinking about the issues rather than hark back to the past or put it down to playing *Übermensch*, as other contemporaries did.

After Merrick had stunned us with his prediction of regular 19-goal matches, a more accurate perception returned. Maybe he did see it all, not just as the ball whizzed past him 13 times in the two matches against Hungary. The contrasts between the two sides and systems did seem a little clearer to Merrick than others; slightly more removed from the maelstrom than his team-mates, he appeared to appreciate the fluidity of the Hungarians in attack. Many contemporary and subsequent commentators on the Magyars focussed on the withdrawn number ten role of Hidegkuti and the problems the English defence had in responding to this, to them, new position, but this was only one specific issue. The comprehensive differences were those brought forward by Merrick – the inaccurate English passing, the fluidity of Hungarian attacks with no set positions, the observation that the Hungarians played as a machine. Merrick's insight was certainly deeper than most, but was anyone really listening to the Birmingham City goalkeeper?

From these observations Merrick brought forward a list of considered recommendations for the FA and the Football League to introduce in order to make the national team more competitive. There were two main long-term policies Merrick proposed as the twin pillars for England achieving a modern, fluid style of play comparable to Hungary. These major arguments were based on what Merrick saw as a need for a drastic response – the need for England to work on a co-ordinated long-term policy based on taking outstanding young players and building the national team around this group with a clear method of play defined.

The second major recommendation by Merrick was a reduction in the number of club matches. He felt there were too many during the season, which prevented international get-togethers and training. Throughout the next six decades of commentary and assessment on the English national team these two major points were raised regularly. In a knee-jerk reaction as regular as clockwork at least one of these two points would be put forward after every poor England performance or terrible result. However, that's not to diminish the perception of Merrick here – some had brought forward these points before, certainly coach Walter Winterbottom had, but it's interesting that a player in the mid-1950s was clear on what was required to progress. Merrick was subtly attacking the process of selectors or indeed selector and the lack of consistency of approach or any sort of plan.

The players and journalists in the 1950s certainly commented regularly on the near endless chopping and changing of personnel in the national team. Apart from Billy Wright and Tom Finney, even Stanley Matthews was dropped on more than one occasion, and many players came and went with little or no explanation. A couple of good league performances and you were in and one poor one in the national team and you were cast out never to be spoken of again. Your surname would be sullied forever on the tongues of the selection committee.

Merrick had further points of interest to make on the overall functioning of the national team. He stressed the need for England to copy certain attributes of Hungarian play – namely always keeping the ball on the ground, adaptability of wingers to come inside and collect the ball, running on angles and paths different from the predictable England wingers and what Merrick termed 'the skilful use of the deadly through ball'. Unfortunately there is no specific explanation as to what he meant by this term, but by arguing that there needed to be a focus on the effective through ball he was concluding that in the English game this was lacking.

Merrick genuinely covered a full range of issues to emphasise the differences in approach between Hungary and England, including points that almost no one from the participatory side raised, such as players' recompense. Merrick was very clear in pointing out how the Hungarian players were treated both financially and in terms of prestige. The delicious irony was that the supposed amateur players of Hungary did a lot better in terms of renumeration and incentives than the professional English players. Almost all England players of this era brought forward the repeated hackneyed phrase that all they wanted was the honour of playing for their country.

However, there are hints and examples that it wasn't as simplistic as that. The players were treated as second- or even third-class citizens by the FA blazers and they knew it. Every book ever written about Stanley Matthews includes the anecdote about when he was queried and refused payment on an expenses claim he put in for a currant bun while waiting for a train carrying the England party. The greatest player in the world in his position for 20 years treated like a schoolboy over a few pennies. Merrick enveloped the issue by stressing how great the incentives were in Hungary for a sportsman which culminated in a high standard of living. Merrick's book was one of the few autobiographies in the first half of the 1950s that explicitly raised the issue of financial reward.

The class-riven structure of English football in 1954 was still dominated by the maximum wage and restrictions on movement of employment. No doubt it must have deeply rankled with international players as they strode out in front of the vast, locked-out crowds of Wembley and Hampden Park that their appearance fee was so small.

Wherever all that money went from the full grounds around the country week in and week out, it certainly didn't go to players and, in most cases, not on the stadiums either. Players only occasionally raised the point in public, but it surely must have drawn extensive commentary in private – just where did all that money go? Despite Merrick being one of very few England players to mention the fact, it must have appeared strange and somewhat frustrating that their communist opponents in their cherry-red shirts seemed to do a lot better on the status and goodies front than everyone in the England team, with the possible exceptions of Matthews and Wright.

Match preparation is another point where Merrick stressed difference, but this was a common conclusion by many of the players and analysts. The point was, apparently explained directly to Merrick by Puskás himself, that in the six-month period between the 6-3 and 7-1 games the Hungarian national team regulars played only six league matches for their respective clubs and had enjoyed a month together in the Egyptian sun. One can imagine how that went down with the England players contesting their league matches in the sleet and snow of Stoke and Manchester.

I See it All came from the fixed point of the panorama behind ten team-mates and 20 outfield players. The goalkeeper is removed from the maelstrom, from what Meisl termed the 'whirl'. One of the oldest tropes in football is the separation of the goalkeeper from the rest of the team, as the only one who can touch the ball with their hands. The super-specialised role has brought an additional sobriquet that all goalkeepers are basically crazy. However, very little has ever been written about the attributes and opportunities this separation gives to the goalkeeper as the watcher of play, the sentinel.

The 6-3 game was Merrick's 17th cap and only the second defeat he played in for England. This earlier consistency had led to his position as number one in 23 of 24 consecutive internationals between November 1951 and his last game, the 1954 World Cup defeat in the quarter-finals to Uruguay. Despite hundreds of professional appearances, his was the lot of goalkeepers the world over for decades. He was remembered for defeats and specific mistakes, the scapegoat of a thousand goals conceded and a hundred defeats. Merrick became known as 'Mr 13' due to the number he conceded against the Hungarians as if the other ten players on the pitch had nothing to do with it. Alf Ramsey, for one, removed himself from responsibility for several goals conceded in the 6-3 match and roundly blamed Merrick by stating that a fluke percentage of goals were scored from long-range shots and should never have gone in. Even the most cursory view of the game can conclude that Hidegkuti's bullet shot in the second minute would still have been a goal if you'd had Yashin, Banks, Shilton, Zoff and Casillas on the goal line together.

It was the same after England's 4-2 defeat to Uruguay in the 1954 World Cup where Merrick was hung out to dry by Winterbottom, 'Merrick was my disaster, nice fellow, strong, good at club level. But for England he sometimes lost his nerve – against Hungary I felt they were stoppable shots, but he got nowhere near them.' The gap in play, tactics, fitness, training, planning and outlook were all diminished and glossed over. If only we had a different man between the sticks. In fact, Ramsey went as far as to name the man who would have stopped everything the Hungarians threw at England from outside the box – Ted Ditchburn, Ramsey's club-mate at Tottenham Hotspur.

Despite being somewhat shafted by Winterbottom and the likes of Ramsey, that in some sort of parallel universe all that needed to have happened to avoid the two colossal defeats to Hungary was a change of goalkeeper, Merrick was almost certainly the best available at the time. The endless conundrum of the international manager – you have what you have and you're stuck with it, in contrast to the top clubs who aren't happy with the level of performance and just go out and replace the player with a new acquisition often at vast cost, the Real Madrid syndrome. Even in almost all World Cup-winning teams there are a couple of players who are only moderately decent in their position and are somewhat fortunate to win their medal. Ramsey's comment that there was a better player waiting in the wings is another consistent trope which regularly raises its head when failure is present. 'If only we'd played person X rather than Y it would have been different.'

In contrast to Winterbottom's and Ramsey's views on Merrick and his apparent incompetence, other contemporary and subsequent commentators took an opposing view to assess the Birmingham City man as a more modern goalkeeper who focussed on fitness. Nat Lofthouse, for one, viewed Merrick in different terms, as a professor on the pitch, with what he termed a scientific approach based around brilliant positional play and a game that had no light-heartedness within it. A goalkeeper whose success and reputation was built on positional play had a new identified challenge with the fluid interchanging positions of the Hungarian team.

The English league system was based on rigidity and fixed positions, runs and angles of play that a clever goalkeeper could learn and predict. The emphasis Merrick placed on the movement of the Hungarians across his view in *I See it All* was clearly what disconcerted him as much as it did Harry Johnston and Billy Wright. Merrick did not appear to have been educated by Winterbottom to expect runs, passes and shots at angles and in areas he was not used to.

Merrick was a reasonably popular figure with the media, with his film star visage and meticulously clipped moustache. He was a photogenic individual whom the contemporary magazines enjoyed writing an article on. *World Sports Magazine* in March 1954 termed Merrick 'the born goalkeeper' as he had wanted to play in the position since the age of eight and had done everything he could in terms of a fitness regime, which was unusual for British players in the 1940s and '50s. Merrick combined his duties as a loyal one-club man at Birmingham with being a sports master in the city, utilising his army PT background and reputation as a fitness fanatic, again not a given in the world of English professional football in 1953.

Merrick reconfirmed that there were three main attributes a goalkeeper must have – a quickness of mind and body, good handling and a fine sense of anticipation. Overall, a very modernistic outlook to goalkeeping. Indeed, this brief list could have been written in the 21st century rather than in a general sports magazine from 70 years ago. Merrick appeared, once again, to be reluctant to mention the 6-3 defeat as it was only four months before the *World Sports* article was written by the journalist Eddie Griffiths. Perhaps the experience was too raw for the exotically named 'blue panther'. Perhaps the dizzying runs and passes of the Hungarian sprites were not fully formed in his mind until after the devastation in Budapest, as one of only four England players, along with Wright, Dickinson and Sewell, to appear in both games. His is the view of the double perspective, in comparison to the single 90-minute discombobulation of Harry Johnston.

Indeed Merrick, a lesson in fitness and consistency with a record 551 league and cup games for the Blues, including 145 consecutive appearances from 1949 to 1952, who was known throughout the game for his methodical and unspectacular play in order to conserve energy by sound positioning, suffered the goalkeeper's curse, the stopper's ultimate humiliation and life burden, as did Barbosa for Brazil in 1950 against Uruguay and as did Peter Bonetti in England's 1970 World Cup quarter-final defeat to West Germany. A whole nation brought down their anger and tumult on a single man and his work performance in a 90-minute period. Hungary didn't scrape two victories in November 1953 and May 1954, they inflicted two of the statistically worst defeats in England's international history. Indeed, the 7-1 annihilation is the worst England defeat in statistical terms and surely will always remain so. The death hammer came down for many after the 6-3 game, but Merrick lasted out to the 1954 World Cup in Switzerland.

Only a few weeks after the Budapest defeat, England lined up against the modern and super-tough Uruguayans, the defending world champions. In a decision by the FA that equalled the lack of planning for the 1950 World Cup, they chose as their final international warm-up game before the 1954 finals to play Hungary in Budapest. 'Look chaps, I've got a great idea. You know that team that destroyed us at Wembley 6-3 last November? Well, why don't we play them at their own new stadium in Budapest 25 days before the World Cup begins as a confidence booster? I know they are basically the best team in the world and have been undefeated for years, but I think it will be good preparation.'

Cconceding seven goals in an England international had happened only once before against Scotland in 1878 and it hasn't happened since. It was also 23 years previously that England had received a tonking off a continental team when they lost 5-2 to France in Paris. The combination of the Budapest debacle and just a month later the Uruguayans putting four past Merrick in Basle meant that the trauma of defeat was squarely laid on his shoulders. The shortcomings of a team were pushed on to one man and Merrick was dropped, never to return to international football.

Alf Ramsey: the General

At right-back, with his slicked-back, jet-black hair was positioned the General, Alf Ramsey. From old Dagenham, according to his entry in the *Oxford Dictionary of National Biography*, his father was a hay and straw dealer, but the rumours within football were always that Ramsey's family were gypsies. Sir Alf, as he became in 1967, always appeared to be overly sensitive and somewhat embarrassed about his background. His attempt to lose his Dagenham accent through elocution lessons, which only made him sound like Parker off *Thunderbirds*, was the clearest example of this. The altered speech patterns reverted to pure Dagenham when a sharp-tongued bollocking was issued for a wayward pass.

Ramsey was a patriot of the utmost degree, which frequently passed over into xenophobia and this regularly manifested itself in some dubious conclusions on match results involving England both as a player and later manager. Ramsey was convinced that England should have comfortably beaten the USA in the 1950 World Cup and, even years later, was still adamant that they should never have lost 6-3 to Hungary in 1953. In what was a common theme for players in the team defeated by Hungary he was quite keen to point the finger of blame elsewhere. Even in later years, when Ramsey was manager of England, Bobby Charlton commented that the 6-3 defeat still rankled with him and he termed it a distortion. He could never fully forget the humiliation suffered at the feet of Hidegkuti and Puskás. Charlton mused that it was a key factor in driving Ramsey and England forward to establish a setup where the team would never be so exposed again.

The problem, as far as Ramsey was concerned, was defence. This was where he targeted his specific negative comments regarding the performances of his team-mates Merrick and Harry Johnston as being the cause for the heavy defeat, and where he later focussed in terms of his own England teams in the 1960s and 1970s. Ramsey was consistently adamant that England could have won that day as four out of the six Hungarian goals were from outside the penalty area, and this should never have happened.

Ramsey was an unusual figure as he appears to have been respected by all his peers. Certainly, at different times he was talked about in effusive terms by Matthews, Wright and Nat Lofthouse. The two main areas that garner respect from his playing contemporaries were his professionalism and that he was a deep thinker about all aspects of the game. Ramsey came to professional football late at the age of 24 and after a spell at Southampton he found a spiritual home with Tottenham Hotspur under the management of Arthur Rowe. Rowe's famous 'push and run' side gained promotion from the Second Division and then won the First Division title in the 1950/51 season, with Ramsey as an integral part of the team. The level of his performances during this period led to his being an absolute fixture in the England national team between December 1948 and November 1953, with a particular run of 28 consecutive appearances, including two as captain when Billy Wright was unavailable.

Tottenham was such an important place for Ramsey because of Rowe. He was Rowe's representative on the pitch. Rowe and Ramsey connected because they were both thinkers of the game with Ramsey taking a position that was the absolute antithesis of Stanley Matthews, that even great players can be more effectively coached and utilised in a preconceived plan. Here was the crux of the split in English football in the early 1950s between those who wanted to preserve the status quo, harking back to a mythical era and those who wanted change and to embrace new ideas. Ramsey wanted to advance and develop the game and his club connection with the peripatetic Rowe was an important part at the beginning of this process. Indeed, there was a direct connection to the 6-3 game as Rowe had previously coached in Hungary.

Ramsey had primarily been a student of his own game which had led to a distinctive style based around him coming to football late and possessing, what was acknowledged by most of his contemporaries, a chronic lack of pace. Ramsey was a more modern full-back in that his game was not just about feeding the ball up to the winger. He worked hard to maximise his potential and developed a strong positional sense, a distinctive hard, low, direct pass which Matthews enjoyed receiving and a calm, unflappable demeanour commented on by everyone. Lofthouse clearly concluded that he saw Ramsey as the best driver of an accurate ball he ever saw.

Ramsey was keen to develop new ways of building up from the back at Tottenham and linked with goalkeeper Ted Ditchburn by encouraging direct distribution to himself via an accurate throw rather than the aimless long kick up the centre of the pitch. Matthews was another definite admirer of Ramsey, stressing the same attributes as Lofthouse – interception, positional play and thinking about the game both on and off the pitch. Matthews held Ramsey in high esteem as he was exactly the type of full-back he didn't like playing against, the calculating individual who bided his time. Wright followed Matthews's theme in his 1953 book *The World's My Football Pitch*, assessing Ramsey as the most remarkable defender he'd ever met. Ramsey's ice-cool persona and thoughtful observations on the game clearly had a considerable impact on Wright.

Ramsey appeared to have initiated a process unusual among players in England at the time – he analysed the game played, often in its immediate aftermath. A particular Ramsey hobby horse of the early 1950s was the 'constructive defence' on which he would espouse to players and journalists alike at regular opportunities. This primarily involved holding on to the ball until good use could be made of it. Such a concept in 1953 English football still required commentary and was deemed innovative enough to include in a published autobiography.

Though Ramsey was known in England as football's intellectual, who apparently thought about soccer tactics as if they were chess problems, it's important to remember where the bar was set for someone to be described as an intellectual within the English football world and that was very low. Despite this point Ramsey was an important figure as a player because he was a core individual involved in thinking and talking about the game, an acolyte of

Winterbottom. Wright appeared to view Ramsey, when still a player, as a similar personality to Winterbottom – calm, a teacher, unflappable, an immaculate individual off the pitch. Perhaps there's a basic truth in the Ironbridge boy's conclusion, perhaps Ramsey deliberately styled himself on Winterbottom down to wanting to change his speaking voice to the more clipped tones of Winterbottom and attend a series of elocution lessons.

Wright stated that Ramsey would talk about football for hours and would act as a catalyst by encouraging his team-mates to come forward with their ideas on the game and improving performance, if they had any. This was effusive praise to a level usually reserved for Winterbottom and concluded that with Ramsey's remarkable outlook and contribution he helped improve the standard of defensive play. Perhaps one of the reasons Wright was so positive about Ramsey was due to his antipathy to Matthews. Wright argued that Ramsey's concept of constructive defence was an entirely new approach to full-back play which brought them into offensive play and contributed towards scoring goals. Wright appeared to take great glee in Ramsey not standing on reputation and, from his first appearance, was ordering Matthews around in terms of positioning. Lofthouse confirmed that Ramsey was a great student of the game and would endlessly discuss football in a manner that Lofthouse found interesting. Clearly important attributes for someone to move into the first wave of coaching managers when he retired from playing.

In the fluctuating world of the selectors Ramsey was a novelty, along with captain Billy Wright, in that he consistently retained his place over a three-season period and held his position as penalty taker for the international side, scoring important spot kicks against Yugoslavia in a 2-2 draw at Wembley, becoming the first continental team to achieve a draw in England, and a highly dubious and late equalising penalty in the exciting 4-4 draw versus the Rest of Europe. In addition, after Robb was rugby tackled to the ground, Ramsey dispatched England's third from the penalty spot against Hungary in November 1953.

Despite his consistency at right-back and featuring in most England internationals in the previous four years, two as captain, it all ended for Ramsey after the 6-3 defeat. Ramsey certainly concluded that others were more responsible than him for the loss. In the core of that argument, he was fundamentally correct, not at pointing the finger directly at Merrick, but that the game was lost in the centre where the Hungarian movement of the 'whirl' dominated the central English players, not out in the position of full-back. How many games are ever actually won or lost due to the performance of the full-back? However, after the catastrophe the selectors' axe fell in a random swathe and one of the numerous heads that was lopped off was Ramsey's. As he walked forcefully off the Wembley pitch already convinced that the result was an undeserved fluke, it was the last time he ever wore the England shirt.

Of course, though Ramsey was a top international player, he is always remembered for his managerial achievement of bringing the World Cup to England in 1966. The foundation stone of his development into coaching and management was his relationship with Walter Winterbottom. In his 1952 autobiography *Talking Football*, Ramsey shared his views on Winterbottom and his role in the England setup. As someone deeply interested in the development of football it was no surprise that Ramsey was almost wholly positive about the work Winterbottom was doing, both as England manager and director of coaching. Ramsey focussed on the point of Winterbottom's preparation, something Ramsey himself later became renowned for, and commented at length on his famous pre-match talks or 'pow-wows' as he termed them. His commentary on the fact that a manager spoke at considerable length, sometimes 90 minutes, to his players before an important game showed how unusual and ground-breaking Winterbottom's approach was.

Ramsey was certainly 100 per cent in the pro-Winterbottom group, stating his great respect for both his knowledge of the game and his communication skills, being able to put over his points in an easy-to-understand and concise manner. Ramsey was interested in the argument of many that because Winterbottom had never been an international-class player and some erroneously believed he'd never been a professional player, therefore, he shouldn't be in a position where he was educating and coaching seasoned international sportsmen.

An area that Ramsey noted Winterbottom specialised in was his knowledge of and preparation around opponents. *Talking Football* was published before the 6-3 game, so Ramsey gave no comment on the controversy of whether Winterbottom prepared the England team for Hungary's specific tactics and team shape or not. He did make the point, though, that it was standard practice for Winterbottom to thoroughly brief the players on their continental opponents – their danger men, methods and even temperament. This was a routine that Ramsey was clearly very struck with before his second international versus Italy in 1949 and this approach persisted over Ramsey's career as an England player. Winterbottom went to see Hungary in their international versus Sweden a month before the 6-3 game, as part of his research, so it would seem very odd that someone who went to these lengths on a regular basis did not inform and prepare the team for what lay ahead with the Hungarians, as some players stated was the case. Another example was in 1951 when Winterbottom flew to Brussels to watch Austria destroy Belgium 8-1 and then to Paris for a 2-2 draw between France and Austria, all in preparation for an international that England had against Austria at Wembley.

For players such as Ramsey, who wanted to know about foreign individuals, teams and tactics, Winterbottom was the fount of all contemporary knowledge. Except for a small coterie of journalists – Brian Glanville, Charles Buchan and Geoffrey Green – very few English people would see or be informed about continental football. Certainly, the avenues for contemporary knowledge for the England players, even if they were interested and some were not, was very limited. Ramsey also appreciated that Winterbottom respected input from players and acted as a chairman in meetings where ideas and a voice would be encouraged in an inclusive manner, far removed from the dictatorial approach of many English club managers down the ages. Ramsey felt his opinion was sought after by Winterbottom and appreciated being able to bring his ideas forward, something he then replicated in his time as England manager.

Billy Wright: the Golden Boy

In the hierarchy of time and words allotted to the 11 England internationals who walked out against Hungary, no one had a more prevalent voice than Billy Wright. Perhaps Stanley Matthews was close, but no one surpassed him. During their careers or immediately into retirement they both produced an incredible four autobiographies but in an interesting divergence since that point in the subsequent decades, multiple biographies of Matthews have been published on a regular basis, but there has only been one full biography on Wright, in 1980.

Whereas Matthews was internationally renowned purely due to his level of skill and the longevity of his career, Wright was primarily famous internationally due to his England career and his captaincy over his 105-cap run. Wright was the first player in international football to play 100 internationals and he captained England a record 90 times, later equalled by Bobby Moore. It was this continual presence in the England team for 13 years which provided the framework for his quartet of autobiographies – *Captain of England* in 1950, *The World is My Football Pitch in* 1953, *Football is My Passport* in 1957 and *One Hundred Caps and all That* in 1962. Wright was not only ubiquitous in the England team between 1946 and 1959 but his presence was everywhere in the English media as the face and voice of everything positive about English football and, indeed, young English manhood.

The golden boy is one of the archetypes of the English national team and the way that particular person is judged is framed by the media. The golden boys were primarily assessed on ability and performance and then personality or behaviour, until behaviour became irrelevant during the era of Paul Gascoigne. Certainly, Wright would have been absolutely mortified at the litany of Gazza's incidents and him remaining untouchable in the team due to his media image. Wright, Bobby Moore, Kevin Keegan, Gary Lineker, Gascoigne, David Beckham, Michael Owen and Wayne Rooney all filled the role at one time or another. The golden boy lived by different rules to every other player with the media interested in a wide range of areas of their private lives – wives, partners, clothes, social lives, cars, holidays and so on. Wright ticked all the boxes for being the golden boy – he was Footballer of the Year in 1952, received a CBE in 1959, and had an unblemished disciplinary record when that was important in shaping an image. The press termed him 'football's boy scout', clean-cut, humble with a smile. Wright was generally admired outside the game for what he had made of his football career. He was not the most naturally gifted of players and it was through individual commitment and devotion that he turned himself into a top-class international. Wright was a fitness fanatic whose greatest single attribute was the consistency of his performance. As a man who practised hard he was singular in his ambition, open to listening to coaching and management, and with particular importance on embracing positional change.

All these points made Wright a true golden boy, perhaps THE golden boy of English football with his wavy blond hair *à la* Tintin and pleasant but rather goofy smile. He wasn't from a big industrial city that myth tells us is where all the top players came from but from the small Shropshire town that acted as the catalyst for the beginning of the Industrial Revolution – Ironbridge, where his father was an iron moulder. The then Tottenham manager Arthur Rowe, according to Glanville, thought Wright was a 'real nana' and this encapsulates a position that some weren't too keen on Wright's total deference bordering on sycophancy to authority figures within the game. His clear position in a hierarchy of Rous, Winterbottom and Wright was apparent to all.

However, the English football world of the early 1950s was strictly hierarchical and mostly deferential. Only a handful of players such as Matthews, Wright and Finney, who were more widely known to the general public, earned a very good living from the £50 England appearance fee and the extras that their profile gave them and, presumably, Wright didn't want to jeopardise this position. Given the endless bizarre decisions of the international selection committee in omitting players for no apparent reason, behaving in a manner that would be even the slightest bit confrontational to the structure could mean permanent banishment from the international team and the extra money that came with it. Perhaps Wright was somewhat duplicitous in his stand on Stanley Matthews but surely there's only ever going to be one winner and one loser if you strongly and publicly criticise a living legend. In a similar point to that made by Wolves manager Stan Cullis, Wright was known to be heavily critical, in the dressing room, of the predictability of Matthews's play and how it slowed down attacks, but in public environments he was never anything but wholly effusive to every aspect of the winger's performances and singularity.

Though Wright had important on-the-pitch associations with players such as Ramsey and Dickinson, the most important relationship that acted as the fulcrum of the international side was that which existed between Wright and manager Walter Winterbottom. Again, other players certainly commented that Wright was nothing more than a lapdog to Winterbottom, but the overall position was much more complicated than this. Players such as Matthews, Raich Carter and Len Shackleton shared a collective view that they had nothing to learn whatsoever from Winterbottom and that they could not and would not be coached. However, Wright was interested in aspects of self-improvement education in general, completing courses in engineering and English at college and listening to classical music. He played almost all his football career under just two managers – Cullis and Winterbottom. Though they thought about football in different terms, they did think about the game and study their own players and opponents. Wright was impressed by Winterbottom from the beginning of their involvement with one another both as a person and for his approach to football and this was to remain the case for the whole of his England career and afterwards.

Wright took Winterbottom's approach off the pitch and made it the cornerstone of how he would play for and captain England. There were three specific points that he based his approach on. He was clear he would not shout at or bully a player on the field, or demonstrate by waving his arms in the air, and would assume the role of football foreman. This was the role Nat Lofthouse saw Billy Wright in, as a liaison officer between the players and Winterbottom and chairman of selectors Harold Shentall, earlier in Wright's position as England captain. Lofthouse emphasises that there was never any unpleasantness, but this is to mis-conclude the relationship. Power was all in the hands of the FA selection committee and, fundamentally, the players had absolutely no power or influence at all. Even Winterbottom's position and role at first was highly limited so the players were most definitely not listened to. You can't really be a liaison officer if all the power and instruction is one way. The position of any player in the international team was potentially precarious, and even the great Stanley Matthews was dropped on several occasions during his long international career.

Those who appeared for England were dictated to in all aspects – what to wear, how to behave, how much they were paid (even as late as the 1950s some in the upper echelons of the FA were still fundamentally opposed to any payments to players appearing for international duty), how they played, where they stayed and what they ate. The international selection committee were not the slightest bit interested in the input or opinion of the players. The players were not under any specific contractual obligation as at their clubs and the highly paternalistic approach should really be termed exactly what it was – master and servant. The framework for the players was one of compliance or non-involvement. The last resort of workers the world over is the removal of labour, but in this context it would have achieved nothing on an individual basis. If you refused to play for England under the conditions dictated to you then your position would just be filled by another, and you would never play again. When the selection committee dropped a player of Matthews's ability and reputation or ruthlessly ended the international careers of stalwarts without a second thought, such as Alf Ramsey or Stan Mortensen, this sent an unequivocal message to all as to who was in charge.

Winterbottom summed up Wright's importance as a player and captain in the 1960 Bob Ferrier book *Soccer Partnership*. He encapsulated Wright as a solid but not spectacular player whose numerous positive attributes included interception, lightning recovery, strong in the air, firm tackling, saying he did not take risks and did the simple things well with a compact style. Wright was a student of the game, the type of player Eric Cantona would later describe in derogatory terms as a water carrier. Winterbottom developed this special relationship with Wright over many years and it was the attributes that Winterbottom saw in Wright which led to his promotion to captain of the international team, replacing George Hardwick and retaining this role for an incredible 90 matches. Winterbottom argued for Wright to be captain due to his experience, high level of sustained performance, dependability and as an on-the-pitch leader in the Winterbottom mould of putting points and ideas across without shouting and screaming.

Due to his high profile at the time, Wright was probably the major public voice and myth-maker of the English experience of the 6-3 game. His points and interpretations became those of many who read his multiple autobiographies and in a myriad of articles and quotes both in contemporary and secondary sources. The opinions of Puskás's tummy, the Hungarian kit, defensive failings, Puskás's roll-back goal and the codifying of the Hungarian players as superhuman were all due to the central presence and comments by Wright. Wright was nothing but completely complementary about the Hungarian team to the point of awe. They were described as *Übermensch*, the German philosopher Friedrich Nietzsche's term of supermen and a zeitgeist word of the mid-20th century. A rather controversial word to use less than a decade after the Nazi domination of Europe, which included the invasion of Hungary. This was an early development of the Hungarians as superbeings, men from another planet who played football of a quality that no one could possibly compete with, though Hungary had drawn their previous international with Sweden 2-2 and would lose the World Cup Final eight months later against West Germany in Switzerland. In many ways Billy Wright set the tone as to how the game was remembered both in 1953 and subsequently.

This remembrance is never more prevalent than in the scoring of Puskás's famous drag-back goal, the third of the match and Puskás first. In a similar level of reporting to the near disbelief of Puskás's keepy-uppies before kick-off, the fascinating aspect of this goal is the tone of how it is repeatedly described. Clearly the near hysteria is a result of its uniqueness at the time in English football. Simply no one had ever seen anything like it. The goal was a nice piece of skill by Puskás, who held the ball and as Wright charged in he rolled it back across his studs, pivoted and slammed it home from close range past a statuesque Merrick.

In the endless commentary on that goal, including from Wright directly, the focus was not on the actual goal but the fool that Puskás made of England's captain. Norman Giller in *Billy Wright: A Hero for All Seasons* stated nearly 30 years after the event that for the rest of his life Wright remained haunted by this classic goal. It was Geoffrey Green who constructed the classic comment on Puskás's move and goal, saying that Wright resembled a fire engine going full speed in the wrong direction. It was this comment that was replayed constantly by commentators and writers to confirm the gap between the skilled, modern technique of the Hungarians and the boneheaded pure physicality of England. The chasm stretched the descriptive process to the maximum of placing the Hungarians in the context of superbeings or visitors from another planet.

The question of preparation and knowledge of the Hungarians before the 6-3 game is, once again, vague and even contradictory. In the final instalment of his career-based autobiographies, *One Hundred Caps and All That*, written with Bryon Butler and published after his international career had ended in 1962, Wright commented that the reputation of the Hungarians had preceded them by several weeks, but if this were the case how does this balance against so many of the England team being surprised at the manner in which Hungary played? According to Wright in his 1957 autobiography *Football is My Passport*, Winterbottom had most definitely flown out to Budapest to watch Hungary versus Sweden along with a small cohort of top football writers from the English press – John Graydon (*Sunday Graphic*), Roy Peskett (*Daily Mail*), Clifford Webb (*Daily Herald*), John Cankin (*News Chronicle*) and Desmond Hackett (*Daily Express*). There was clearly preparation and expense laid out to facilitate this trip, so how did this not communicate itself to players on the pitch being prepared? Wright even stated that over a breakfast in Vienna, Winterbottom had Sweden's English manager George Raynor draw up a plan which he had used to hold Hungary in their international. Wright also reinforced that the interest in England for the Hungarian team was unparalleled, particularly after England had been held by the FIFA select team the previous month. This was an interesting way of wording the 4-4 draw with FIFA as it was England who managed to scrape the draw with a highly fortuitous penalty converted late in the game by Alf Ramsey.

Wright didn't focus exclusively on the explanation of Hungary's supremacy being due to Hidegkuti as the withdrawn number ten, as so many commentators contemporary and subsequent claimed. He saw the Hungarian dominance as more complete than just one specific tactical change. The key factors for Wright were the precision passing and movement, mixing up the short and long passes with imagination and accuracy. This precision of understanding could only be developed with a combination of players with a high level of individual skill who trained and played together on a consistent basis to merge their skills into a highly effective unit.

Wright was one of the key English participants and assessors, present in the centre of the pitch and at the core of play where he experienced the maelstrom of the Hungarian whirl all around him. In terms of defensive tactics Wright was clear that the system talked through beforehand was that of the retreating defence, where the defensive grouping held their line and submitted the opposition to retaining possession. Wright contended that there were two main factors as to why Hungary won so convincingly – first was the consistently argued point that Hungary were so effective because they were two club sides merged into one team and who just wore a different shirt and trained and played together far more regularly than the English national team, which was unquestionably the case.

The second point that Wright argued was one he mentioned on a couple of occasions in his autobiographies, that England were beaten because the contemporaneous English youth of 1953 was too busy being distracted by the impact of postwar material consumption on their leisure time. In the interwar self-perceived halcyon childhood of Wright's generation, the only option was football. The increase in leisure goods in the postwar period meant that there was too much time spent watching television (still not present in the majority of homes in the early 1950s), cinema and listening to the radio whereas the Hungarian youth had no such options. Of course, this simply wasn't true; television was not a consumerist product owned by many in communist Hungary but radios and cinema-going were both highly popular. In addition was the fundamental paradox Wright argued, that the reason England's pinnacle players failed was due to boys and teenagers going to the cinema.

There is no question that Wright and Winterbottom had a long and special relationship as manager and captain. It was Winterbottom as the newly appointed and first national team manager who oversaw the young and raw Shropshire lad Wright coming into the international setup in 1946. It was Winterbottom who was there right through Wright's extraordinary career until 1959, 105 caps later. Though Winterbottom regularly and clearly praised Wright in his performance and attitude it was always measured and thought through in his typical manner, certainly never overly effusive. Wright, however, was almost endlessly complimentary about Winterbottom to the point of sycophancy, seeing him as a guide, mentor and trailblazer, who was the fount of all knowledge. He was an even stronger advocate for Winterbottom and his ideas than Alf Ramsey.

In his first autobiography from 1950, *Captain of England*, Wright had already argued that Winterbottom was fundamentally flawless in his approach and role with some statements in direct contradiction of many other players who appeared for England under Winterbottom's long tenure. A constant point made by many players from Tommy Lawton to Bobby Charlton was that Winterbottom was too much of a schoolteacher and a boffin for the professional football world. Wright held the completely opposite view that Winterbottom 'never struck me as possessing the mannerisms that are so often spotted in a man who has been a schoolmaster'. This seems a somewhat extraordinary claim as Winterbottom had been a teacher and certainly saw his role of developing the national coaching structure as fundamentally teaching. In every picture from the 1950s of Winterbottom he looks exactly like a younger schoolmaster teaching, guiding and encouraging his pupils.

The hagiographic approach of Wright to Winterbottom can be quite draining to read across page after page of his four autobiographies spanning a 12-year publishing period. Winterbottom filled numerous roles and positions for Wright, but according to his captain Winterbottom was infallible. Wright was used to a club manager who thought about the game and who developed his own approach in Stan Cullis. The outlook of Cullis and Winterbottom was very different overall but in some ways they were similar as they tried to break away from the old staid approach where training and matches were fundamentally the same week after week.

Wright confirmed Ramsey's assessment of Winterbottom that he knew the game inside and out and focussed on two attributes that Winterbottom brought to his position – that he was inclusive in his approach with discussions and brought players' voices forward to be heard, and the introduction of team tactical discussions regarding upcoming opposition. Of course, both Ramsey and Wright engaged in these processes and appreciated that their opinions and input were sought. However, Wright did make crucial claims that are difficult to accept. In *Captain of England*, he argued, 'Walter Winterbottom has the deep respect of all who have been associated with him as members of England's international soccer team.' This was most definitely not the case as several prominent players, mostly notably from the previous generation of internationals, such as Lawton and Matthews, fundamentally did not respect Winterbottom at all or the new methods that he was introducing. Stanley Matthews was open about his negative opinion of Winterbottom and coaching in general.

In his last autobiography as a player from 1962, Wright looked back on the process of Winterbottom's dual role in charge of the national team and developing a national coaching structure. He argued that by the early 1960s Winterbottom's talents were being appreciated more by an increasing number of people. By 1962 Winterbottom had directly coached either as England manager or through his FA coaching courses a whole generation of motivated players. Many of these early attendees at the FA courses formed the cohort of the new coaching-based managers in English league football – the likes of Dave Sexton, Bobby Robson and Malcolm Allison.

In Wright's assessment, he made the fascinating point that Winterbottom should be revered in the history of English football in the same manner as Vittorio Pozzo in Italy or Gusztáv Sebes in Hungary. For a very long time this was not the case, perhaps partly due to England's success in 1966 which was just four years after he left his post as national manager and him being overshadowed by his ex-player and student, Alf Ramsey. The rehabilitation of Winterbottom has become firmly established with his statue at the FA's national headquarters at Burton-on-Trent and a full and expansive biography by Graham Morse. The more accurate conclusion is that we must look on Winterbottom's broad achievements, particularly his role as the driving force for the establishment of a national football coaching programme, rather than just his position as England national manager.

Wright looked back from his 1962 autobiography to 1953 and 1954 as a crux in the role of Winterbottom and his attempts to introduce a gradual change to the England setup. He acknowledged that the levels of resistance to change from several different quarters was an important factor as to why tactics were outmoded in England at club and international levels. In 1953 Wright had been highly accurate in his assessment of the long road ahead for Winterbottom in attempting to effect positive change. Wright certainly identified the simple lack of time available to the national coach to implement his coaching and tactical explanations. Fundamentally you can have all the interesting and new programmes you want, but if your players aren't around to engage in the process then its impact will be limited. Wright stressed the disadvantage of Winterbottom having to try and mould players from Manchester United, West Bromwich Albion, Wolverhampton Wanderers, Tottenham Hotspur, Birmingham City and Aston Villa who played in varying systems and setups, whereas other countries in the 1950s, most notably Hungary and Brazil, would have their international squads together for much longer periods of time. Wright pointed out that often Winterbottom would not even be able to hold a post-match debrief due to many of his players leaving immediately after an international to return to their clubs.

The importance of the double Hungarian defeats to England was, looking back ten years later, that they were the catalyst for the biggest, most critical examination and reassessment the game in England had probably ever known. Wright was somewhat naive and inaccurate on this point. The supertanker was slowly turning beforehand but the inquiries were a knee-jerk reaction and, certainly in the press, faded away quite quickly. More important developments were in the already established coaching programmes where younger players, including near-future internationals such as Don Howe and Bobby Robson, attended and learned Winterbottom's tactical and coaching techniques in depth and over a longer period of time.

When the new wave of players came into the England squad over the mid-to-late 1950s, they were already informed and comfortable with Winterbottom and his ideas and the presence of coaching at the highest level wasn't the complete culture shock it had been for players from the interwar generation of Matthews, Lawton and to a lesser extent Wilf Mannion. Wright was confident that though the Hungarians were a superb team who easily beat England at Wembley, the claims by many that they played a totally new form of the game was nonsense. According to Wright, all the Hungarians had done was recycle major principles of the English game from the interwar period. He also argued that those who praised the Hungarians for being so innovative had not been watching Tottenham Hotspur over the previous few seasons as they played in a style which was similar to Hungary with faster movement off the ball.

Wright as the golden boy of his generation was one of only three players from the 6-3 defeat whose international career fully survived. He and Jimmy Dickinson were the only two players who were definite fixtures a year later, while Stanley Matthews continued his rather oblique pattern of runs in and out of the team. Wright survived mostly by being adaptable with a positional change from Winterbottom to centre-half. This move came after the quarter-final defeat to Uruguay in the 1954 World Cup. This change in role went hand in hand with a change in Wright's perspective and a broadening of horizons.

This can be exemplified by assessing Wright's selections in his World XIs, a staple of footballers' biographies and fans across the world and through time. A chapter on a player choosing their World XI was a standard page filler and an opportunity to rhapsodise in autobiographies for decades. Wright's first select XI chosen in 1953 for *The World's My Football Pitch* showed a quite spectacular level of insularity. Of the 13 players picked, 12 were British – comprising nine Englishmen, two Welshmen and a Scot, leaving just one place for a non-British player, Gerhard Hanappi of Austria.

Wright and England's more expansive approach during the 1950s resulted in a much more cosmopolitan select team that appeared in 1962's *One Hundred Caps and All That*. There was still a strong British selection with Englishmen Frank Swift, Duncan Edwards, Stanley Matthews, Wilf Mannion and Tom Finney, and Welshman John Charles. However, now the team was half foreign with two Brazilians, Djalma Santos and Nilton Santos, the Argentine Alfredo Di Stéfano and two Hungarians from the *Aranycsapat* – Ferenc Puskás and Wright's man of the match from the 6-3 game, József Bozsik.

A broader range of international opponents, World Cups and established European club competitions led to an increased regular and continual contact and appreciation of players from Europe and South America. Wright put this altering perspective succinctly when he wrote in the 1950s, 'I quickly realised something few people at home appreciate, and that is – football is now played by more countries than any other sport.' He later added, 'When Britain ruled as kings of football they were about the only people playing the game. Now the whole world plays association football and having taken the game with the seriousness that was once ours, have in many instances, passed us as serious exponents of the game.'

By 'the whole world' Wright basically meant Europe and Latin America. This statement probably could have been written 20 years earlier but finally a player involved in the England setup realised that the position of England and the continuing development of a global game meant that the outlook could never return to what it had been. Nothing could encapsulate this growth and clash of perspectives more than the absolute incredulity with which Wright described that in Brazil it was possible to buy football boots for a four-year-old. The diametrically opposed outlook with presumably quite wealthy Brazilians, buying specific little lightweight football boots for their four-year-old son, and English professional players still using the huge, toe-capped working boots with studs banged in was clear for all to see.

Throughout his playing career and later in life Wright's admiration for and appreciation of the Hungarian teams of the 6-3 and 7-1 matches never diminished. He became close personal friends with Puskás and openly stated that a more accurate scoreline should have been 10-3 rather than 6-3. Wright appeared to have been a deeply reflective person who genuinely took time to evaluate the impact of the Hungarians years afterwards. Their performances remained golden and for him they were always the team that played the greatest football he'd ever experienced.

Wright even concluded that though England were destroyed in both games it was, for him, a great honour to be in close proximity to the *Aranycsapat* before it was broken up in the aftermath of the defeat in the 1954 World Cup Final and then the mayhem of the 1956 Hungarian uprising.

Harry Johnston: the One-Club Man

In the England line-up versus Hungary in November 1953 was, inevitably, the person who took more of the blame than anyone else that day, not just for the defeat but for its nature. His name was Harry Johnston. The Blackpool captain was part of a quartet from the Lancashire coastal town who provided a focus for continuity, particularly in attack with Stanley Matthews, Stanley Mortensen and Ernie Taylor. This favouring of the Tangerines was clearly connected to their victory in that May's FA Cup Final. The 6-3 Hungary match and the so-called Matthews Final stood in clear contrast to one another. Six months apart in time, but a universe apart in memory. One a central positive theme and a zenith of club wing play and the other the nadir of experiences for some and the beginning of the process of change.

Before his recall to the England fold in the summer of 1953 for the tour of South America, Johnston had only played for the national team once in six years. In a selection pattern repeated on numerous occasions to multiple players, there appeared no logical process to Johnston's international career. After a debut in an 8-2 victory over the Netherlands in 1946 and an appearance in the 1947 England v Scotland game which ended in a draw, Johnston was then dropped for four years until defeat to Scotland in 1951. Then he was out again for two years until an international run based on the afterglow of his performance in the 1953 FA Cup Final victory, where Johnston played in seven out of eight internationals, only missing the 4-4 draw against the FIFA Rest of Europe team.

Forever linked with these two games in 1953 and the highs and lows they brought, Johnston was assessed in both as the honest English yeoman, one in his element and one completely out of his depth, flailing and waving his arms about in confusion and consternation. He was widely respected within the game by his fellow professionals and was the 1950/51 Football Writers' Association Footballer of the Year. He was held in high esteem as a gentleman of the game who never lost his composure on the pitch, which makes his gesticulations against Hungary all the more extraordinary.

In a similar context to Matthews, Johnston looked nothing like a top-class professional sportsman. He was 34 at the time of the 6-3 game, but he looked closer to 44 – with his thinning and receding hair his appearance was more attuned to that of a tobacconist or a newsagent. Johnston and Matthews were born in 1919 and 1915 respectively and their childhoods and youths through the 1920s and 1930s and the economic hardships and austerity, with Johnston also serving in World War Two in North Africa, showed in their visage in an age before the National Health Service.

In Johnston's autobiography, *The Rocky Road to Wembley*, one section is quoted in many subsequent assessments of the Hungary game and the English national team, that Johnston 'felt utter helplessness of being able to do anything to alter the grim outlook'. Merrick saw the Hungarians flitting and dancing, some with the ball, some without, but Johnston was in the centre of the maelstrom. Johnston stated that one of his major problems was that he was regularly being pulled out of position due to having to move across to support the full-backs who were run ragged by the interchanging Hungarian wide players. The interesting and confusing point here is regarding preparation or, indeed, the lack of it.

Johnston's exasperations in the first half were apparent but he said that Billy Wright tried to assuage his concerns by stressing 'leave it until half-time when Winterbottom will sort it out'. However, crucially, at half-time Winterbottom did not focus on Hidegkuti and his positioning but, apparently, spent most of the interval talking to George Robb. In terms of preparation for the 6-3 match Winterbottom stated that he specifically met with Johnston beforehand to discuss how they were going to deal with the threat from Hidegkuti and concluded that the most effective approach would be to replicate Sweden's system and not follow him around the pitch but leave him to roam in space in front of the defence.

Johnston stated that though the regular English football supporter had very little opportunity to see and appreciate foreign players and teams, it came as no surprise to him that these men with the funny names, as he described them – Puskás and Hidegkuti – could play football and play it brilliantly. Though this was most certainly a valid point it's important to remember the overpowering insularity of the average English football fan in the early 1950s. Even if you were a young man genuinely interested in the European or world game, how would you access any information on football in Hungary or Italy? The idea of a working-class 20-year-old lad from Stoke-on-Trent getting on a plane and flying out to watch Roma v Lazio in 1951 was preposterous: too expensive, impractical and beyond the terms of reference. There was no coverage of European football on television, radio or at the cinema, the influential magazine *World Soccer* didn't start until 1960 and there was almost nothing in the newspapers.

The only, limited, source of football information even of the major European leagues was in articles in publications such as *World Sports Magazine*, edited by Willy Meisl.

Despite Johnston's statement about the utter helplessness he felt during the match, he was a reflective and thoughtful man who, like Merrick, and in contrast to Matthews, brought forward ideas and views as to what had happened in the 6-3 defeat and what England's response should be. Precision was what Johnston recognised as the core to Hungary's game, a precision of movement and passing, which did not waste the ball and possession. Johnston argued that this short passing game and possession-based play was taught by English coaches and, therefore, attempted to diminish the achievement by connecting it back through time with England. Johnston appeared to become somewhat obsessed with Hungary's possession-based performance. England needed to focus on this approach if they were to compete in the modern game with movement off the ball as important as on-the-ball skills – running into open space so players were in the correct position to receive possession. None of Johnston's points were revolutionary and he was at pains to emphasise that the 'whirl' and the mixed-up game of intricate close passing and the occasional long ball were from previous English eras. Johnston called for a bit of a reset in the English game away from all 'the mad greyhound stuff of men chasing passes they haven't a hope of catching'. The precision work and pass were the crux in order to pull a man out of position and instigate what Johnston termed 'the true speed of the game'.

Johnston offered a range of resolutions for England to return to 'soccer supremacy'. This type of term was used regularly by the players and journalists of 1953 and 1954. It was indicative of the assumption that England sat, until that day, at the peak of world football. The conclusion was one that bred nothing but confusion. How could supremacy ever be judged? When England went on their first European tour in the summer of 1908 and in the space of eight days played internationals in Vienna, Budapest and Prague to defeat Austria 6-1 and 11-1, Hungary 7-0 and Bohemia 4-0, then one can only reach a conclusion of supremacy no matter how long ago the matches took place. However, this was 45 years before and while the picture of European and world football had changed dramatically since then, most of those involved in the game in England hadn't realised it.

Johnston had his own very specific ideas of how England could return to the top, but rather than reaching out to at least some new developments as Merrick suggested he moved to a form of retrenchment and returned to a focus on standards within English league clubs. He was fundamental in his view of the creation of a minister of sport, saying he was against it. 'Do we need a soccer Führer?' Johnston asked in mid-20th-century language, relating to a supreme boss who would have responsibility over all resources and players so that England could beat the world. The Blackpool captain did not imagine any such diktat could be useful and instead stressed a need to focus on the Football League and FA Cup.

This seemed an extraordinarily strange statement as in 1953 there was no European Cup, European Cup Winners' Cup, Inter-Cities Fairs Cup, League Cup or European Nations Championship. England had qualified for their only World Cup via the British Home International Championship and played a total of three games at the 1950 tournament. What could Johnston have meant by stating that England should concentrate more on the only two competitions that existed? England's national team salvation was through the league clubs and if the standard of play was raised in the league, then the standards of top players would improve and, therefore, the national team would also progress. Johnston argued the exact opposite to Merrick by stating it would be chaos if the best players were 'creamed off', to use his term, to create a super squad. Presumably Johnston meant chaos for the top league clubs who would be bereft of key players for considerable parts of the season. The only true way to make English players internationals was through league experience.

Almost all of the 11 English players who were defeated in the 6-3 game had considerable league experience, but Johnston saw this focus as the way forward for England – a near isolationist policy which was in direct opposition to the 'futurists' of Winterbottom or Rous who valued engagement and absorption of new ideas in coaching and tactics as the focus for positive development. Johnston then entered the realms of borderline fantasy by concluding that the Hungarians were not particularly skilful players and 'that no one in the Hungarian forward line could as an individual player, trick you with the ease of Mannion, Hagan, Shackleton, Finney or Matthews'. Considering Johnston's extremely close physical proximity to Puskás's famous drag-back goal, it was an astonishing statement, along with rating Puskás as not as clever a player as Shackleton. In Johnston's argument the Hungarians' success was solely based on teamwork and coaching was bordering on a crime. Fundamentally a completely bizarre argument in stating that the only reason, in a team sport, one team was better than another team was because they exhibited better teamwork and played as a unit.

Johnston's other area of complaint and concern, in a similar vein to Billy Wright, was to blame the youth. Wright took a more general approach of unfocussed and wasteful young people in the country. However, Johnston was more specific in his attributing issues in English football to a specific group of people. Termed the 'tragedy of English football', Johnston laid the responsibility of a lowering of standards in the English game on young lads who had great potential who had been written up as international players before they were ready. That comment also included a negative assessment of journalists, but it is extremely difficult to assess what Johnston meant by this as he didn't give any examples. He regarded it as the fault of those at the beginning of their professional journey as players that those at the pinnacle of the game had been destroyed by the Hungarians. Certainly, this conclusion cannot be drawn against the team who lost to Hungary, which was full of experienced internationals – Matthews, Wright, Ramsey, Mortensen – or other experienced league players with hundreds of games under their belt, such as Johnston or Eckersley.

Johnston's scrutiny of Hungary remained in a world of one as he turned his specific analysis to a negative conclusion of one player – Ferenc Puskás. Puskás, scorer of two at Wembley and two in Budapest six months later. Puskás, scorer of 84 international goals in 85 games. Puskás, a player from the pantheon, who came down from Mount Olympus to combine with his comrades at Honvéd and Hungary, who lost his tummy to team up with the original *galáctico* Di Stéfano and take European football to another level in Madrid. Harry Johnston, the yeoman of the guard, had a considerably different opinion of one of the greatest European players of all time.

In what became a common theme in Johnston's autobiography, Puskás was represented as a one-trick pony who ranked way below several England players both past and present from a 1950s perspective. Johnston placed Shackleton, Hagan and Mannion above Puskás for sheer football skill, and from earlier times Raich Carter, Alex James and David Jack were also ranked higher. Puskás was acerbically described as 'just another good inside-forward who showed the fans nothing new'. Johnston concluded that former Northern Ireland international Peter Doherty, in particular, was a player he rated way above Puskás.

The parochialism of Johnston's outlook was re-emphasised with some comments of a beautiful naivety. One of the reasons put forward for the failure was that England's players had to play in all weather conditions of snow, hail, frost and fog, which influenced their style with a focus on strength and power to initiate an effective game plan on heavy, sodden, muddy pitches. England were playing Hungary on that foggy November day, not a select XI from the beaches of Goa. The harshness of mid-continental winters appeared to be an unknown to Johnston.

The conclusion of Johnston's thoughts on the future development of English club and international teams was stark. He argued that there were only two incompatible paths to choose from. Path one was to scrap the existing league structure and instigate a reduced programme and introduce soccer schools where young players are taught to play as a unit in a flow-through structure where the pinnacle is the full international side. The only other option, path two, according to Johnston, was to retain the league as it was, improve the standard of play at clubs and create a considerable pool of world-class players for the international selectors to choose from. A base of two or three world-class players in every position and then just picking the in-form player for each position. In the worldwide history of football has there ever been a country or system that has ever produced a pool of three world-class players in every position to then select one from? The absolute answer is no.

Johnston welcomed the Hungarian performances, even though he felt they were overrated both as a team and as individuals. They had knocked England out of their complacency and presented a challenging situation to all of British football, and should have been applauded for tearing aside the 'complacency and palsy' that had affected the defence-minded game in England. Though Johnston countered this attribute by reiterating that there was nothing world-shattering about the way Hungary played and that originally, they were taught by English coaches anyway, so that brought the Hungarians back into the fold – all they knew and all they learned was from Englishmen, and as Johnston interestingly put it, 'The object of Hungarian play was the same as laid down by our fathers and their fathers before them.'

There are only so many ways to play and they all come back round again – Gusztáv Sebes just stole the 'whirl' from Hugo Meisl's 1930s Austria and what was the Total Football of the 1970s of the Dutch or West Germany than a tweak and subtle re-invention of the whirl? In essence all players stand in a chain, all the way back to the true amateurs of the 1860s praised by Sir Frederick Wall in his autobiography *50 Years of Football*, through to the rise of professionalism and the endless cogent stream of players and talent who connect and play with and against one another – how Stanley Matthews's career ended just as Peter Shilton's began, the goalkeeper later playing against Ryan Giggs in the early 1990s.

Johnston's positive reputation was built on his club career, not his limited international experience. His thinning, combed-back hair in the central pitch positions showed a thoughtful player, not focussed on the huge boot to clear the lines but a more valued pass. He was against the long-ball game, describing it as 'spiv soccer' which sold the supporter short. Johnston played his career in the creative quadrant of the game between wing-half and inside-forwards and regularly emphasised the importance of attractive football, to be achieved by a mixture of short and long passing. He was a player of the maximum wage era who did not focus his energies on securing a bigger slice of the financial pie for players from the colossal gates of the 1940s and 1950s, but more on building a trade or bourgeois career for life after football, usually in the realms of learning a trade or running a shop or pub.

Johnston was a further trope of his time in terms of being a one-club man, as were so many of the 6-3 team, such as Wright, Dickinson and Merrick, who were endlessly described as loyal to their club. Perhaps they were genuinely loyal, perhaps they weren't. The question for men such as Johnston was what was the option but to be loyal to one specific club? Under the almost feudal working conditions of professional footballers before the Professional Footballers' Association, under Jimmy Hill, started to change things to the advantage of the players in the early 1960s, the twin yoke of lack of freedom of employment and the maximum wage meant that there was little motivation on a personal level to seek out employment elsewhere. Even the greatest players of the era – Matthews and Finney – and the greatest financial draws had considerable difficulties even engaging in talks when other employment opportunities presented themselves.

Most players, even in the top division, stayed at one club for 400 games because they had to and what was the motivation to leave if your employment terms and wages were exactly the same somewhere else? Johnston's long Blackpool career lasted from 1937 to 1955 with a period serving in the military in the Middle East during World War

Two. His 438 appearances for the club remained the record until Jimmy Armfield surpassed it and inherited Johnston's sobriquet 'Mr Blackpool'.

The controversy of Johnston's match positioning has confused writers and commentators since the 6-3 game finished. The questions revolve around whether Johnston was instructed to play in a certain position, which he didn't follow, or did he not receive these instructions? Winterbottom was clear that the team had discussed Hungary, not just the so-called deep-lying centre-forward role of Hidegkuti, but the movement and positional interchange of the Hungarian forwards. They had decided to play the retreating defence and let the Hungarians come on to them when in possession of the ball. So why did Johnston feel in the match the need to move into space and mark and challenge Hidegkuti?

Leo McKinstry, in his biography of Sir Alf Ramsey, was scathing that Johnston was the perfect example of England's bewilderment, 'Who had not a clue how to deal with Hidegkuti. If he tried to go with Hidegkuti then he left space for other Hungarians. But if he stayed in defence, Hidegkuti was free to act as playmaker.' It seems difficult to understand why as intelligent and experienced a player as Johnston didn't follow the plan, if indeed there was a plan. To implement the retreating defence inevitably leads to a surrendering of possession. As Puskás said, the major factor to Hungary's victory was movement, so much of it off the ball, not the rigidity and positional misgivings of a single England player. Despite the considerable confusion and contradictory points made by Johnston about the 6-3 game he always maintained that he was pleased and proud to have played in that particular encounter. He felt that the England team did well to score three against Hungary on the day and they weren't disgraced.

Jimmy Dickinson: the Quiet Man

You have to admire the writer Peter Jeffs for bringing together enough information for a biography on Jimmy Dickinson – *Pompey's Gentleman Jim*. Even though it's a rather slim 92 pages, it's quite an achievement. Dickinson may well have 100 per cent deserved his moniker of 'gent' for he never seemed to have commented on anyone or anything in a challenging or, perhaps, negative manner in his entire life. Indeed, he appeared to have gone through his entire adult life without making any single comment of interest on any topic whatsoever.

In many ways Dickinson's England career was a paradox. There were only three survivors a year after the 6-3 defeat. Six of that team never played for England again, Merrick lasted until the 1954 World Cup and Jackie Sewell was brought back for the calamitous 7-1 in Budapest then permanently dropped. Matthews, Wright and Dickinson were the only three who played on under Winterbottom and the slow, sure changes that he phased into the national team. Paradoxical, as Dickinson and Wright were occupants of the 'zone of chaos' where England struggled so deeply to interpret and control the Hungarian movement. Indeed Dickinson, along with Wright, appeared in all three of England's supra defeats of the early 1950s – USA 1950 and the two against Hungary. In addition, he completed an unwanted quartet of horror results as he was also in the team that lost 1-0 to the Republic of Ireland at Goodison Park in 1949. This was England's first home defeat to a foreign – but later redefined as not fully foreign – country.

In November 1953 Wright and Dickinson had played together in the half-back line more than 30 times. Indeed, the match programme clearly stated that their role was the most important in the team as Wright and Dickinson had to gain control of the vital central areas of Wembley, 'blanketing' the Hungarian insiders and linking with their own attack. This control of the central position did not happen and Dickinson didn't attempt to make excuses or deeply analyse the 6-3 result, as others did. He didn't fundamentally try to remove himself from responsibility and by implication blame his team-mates. Indeed, he concluded that, overall, England had been fortunate that the Hungarians had not scored double figures. Skill levels and tactics of the Hungarians were superior to anything Dickinson experienced in the Football League. Decision-making and pass selection were also deemed to be far in advance of what happened in England. Whereas English players would have resorted to the time-honoured response of putting a boot through it – route one or row Z – the Hungarians used their skills to play their way out of a situation.

Dickinson appeared to have been a player caught somewhere between the two camps regarding coaching – the adopters and the rejectors, with perhaps a foot on either side. Dickinson liked and respected Winterbottom, reflecting like many that Winterbottom was more a schoolteacher or scientist than a football man. He was encouraged by Winterbottom to quicken his on-the-pitch thinking and speed up his reactions. Though Dickinson was, perhaps, slowly and surely brought into the pro coaching fold by Winterbottom and his theorist approach, he did sometimes find him too erudite.

Dickinson commented that he was never actually completely sold on coaching. However, his actions and choices between the 1950 and 1954 World Cup told a slightly different story. In Brazil there was the farce of England's campaign from the ridiculous hotel choice in Rio de Janeiro to the embarrassing £2-a-day pocket money for the players and the incomparable defeat in Belo Horizonte to the USA, through to new experiences in the 1953 South American tour with the brilliant Uruguayan Juan Alberto Schiaffino destroying Dickinson, Wright and Johnston in Montevideo. All these performances showed that the approach had to change. Moving on to the Hungary matches, Dickinson stated that he was an admirer of their technique and positional sense, the products of coaching, particularly how they could trap a ball on their chests, thighs and instep in tight areas of the pitch.

Jeffs stated that the manner of the 6-3 defeat challenged Dickinson's whole coaching philosophy, but it's very difficult to interpret what that philosophy was due to a lack of communication on the matter. The manager at Portsmouth did re-look at the tedium of training, but what Dickinson's input was to this is unknown. Interestingly, Jeffs rather bizarrely argued that a considerable mitigating factor for the 6-3 defeat was the presence of too many inexperienced players in the team that day, with poor old George Robb singled out. The England line-up that November day may have been idiosyncratic and wanting, but not inexperienced. Merrick, Ramsey, Wright, Dickinson, Matthews, Eckersley and Mortensen were all experienced international players and it was, mostly, in their areas of the pitch where the issues were present. The forward line, as previously mentioned, was where inexperience was present with Taylor and Robb on cap one and Sewell on cap five, but this was the part of the team that could say they did their job with a considerable role in the three England goals scored. The consistent theme was of describing the Hungarians as supermen or magical by Jeffs with an elevation of their skills and organisation to a level beyond normality and that Jimmy Dickinson was unfortunate to be on the pitch against such superbeings. The same superbeings who had drawn their previous international 2-2 to George Raynor's well-organised Sweden.

However, by the following May in Budapest, Dickinson took the position that he was disappointed by what he perceived as a lack of planning from Winterbottom for the huge task the England team faced. By the time of the Switzerland World Cup a month later Jimmy was so keen to learn new footballing outlooks and developments that, along with Winterbottom and Wright, he stayed to watch the remainder of the tournament and what he saw convinced him that there needed to be a thorough review of the whole attitude to the game in England.

Bill Eckersley: the Invisible Man

Fundamentally, most of history has been the recordings of the life of the powerful and the rich – kings and queens, presidents and prime ministers, generals and admirals, industrialists and explorers. Only relatively recently has social history introduced the voices of the other 99 per cent to bring us the experiences and lives of women, the poor or the foot soldier. The recording of football is no different from any other area in this conundrum. The voice through mediums such as biography and autobiography has been given mostly to the superstar players. For generation after generation the half-baked views and mind-numbing anodyne responses of some selected players has been recorded primarily because they were famous.

The 6-3 team shows this in microcosm with the multiple, contemporary autobiographies of Matthews and Wright juxtaposed against the lack of voice, other than snippets or even semi-snippets from other English players on the pitch that day, most notably Bill Eckersley, but to a lesser extent Ernie Taylor and George Robb. Indeed, for every word written about full-back Eckersley there has been approximately a million written about Matthews or Wright.

There's always a forgotten man in any team. The individual who appears to have had fundamentally no voice at all from the 6-3 defeated team was Eckersley. Sources draw a near blank on his views of the monumental game, in complete contrast to individuals such as Matthews or Ramsey. In all the autobiographies of other England players that appeared around this time, only Alf Ramsey mentioned Eckersley and that was only to say he was full of wisecracks and had a terrific personality.

Although Eckersley had no recorded input on Hungary, England or his own performance at Wembley he was one of six players immediately dropped after the match and one of six players never to play for England again. This was a paradoxical decision by the selection committee to send both full-backs, Ramsey and Eckersley, into international oblivion but to retain players in the central positions such as Wright and Dickinson. Hungary, fundamentally, did not destroy England because they had two orthodox wingers such as Matthews and Finney, who bamboozled the full-backs repeatedly to put in pinpoint crosses to central strikers. The Hungarians won because they completely dominated the central positions of the pitch with their neat passing and positional fluidity causing considerable difficulties for Wright, Johnston and Dickinson. Eckersley's dismissal from the international team appears particularly harsh and, as was so often the case, inexplicable. The 6-3 match was his 17th full international and he had established himself from April 1951 onwards as England's left-back – playing in eight consecutive matches in 1953 including in the tour of South America, and at 27 years of age he was at the peak of his playing years. In a consistent theme of the 6-3 England team, Eckersley was not born in one of the perceived strongholds of footballing talent but in Southport and, similar to Ramsey, was renowned on the pitch for his calm demeanour and his accurate distribution of the ball, fundamentally placing his clearances.

Stanley Matthews: the Incomparable

Stanley Matthews was not incomparable as a player, but as a legend and a myth who moved to god-like status during the course of his extraordinarily long playing career. During that time and afterwards all the premier football writers of his era ran out of superlatives – the 'Wizard', the 'Wizard of the Dribble' and the 'Maestro'. Matthews was revered to a level almost impossible to understand in a media-saturated world where David Beckham was presented as the best player in the world when the reality was that he was the fourth-best player in the classic Manchester United midfield including Roy Keane, Ryan Giggs and Paul Scholes.

Not only did the writers and assessors of the game, such as Geoffrey Green and Ivan Sharpe, run out of gushing prose, the game itself ran out of awards for Matthews – the first Footballer of the Year in 1947, the first European Footballer of the Year in 1956 and the first player to receive a knighthood in 1965. However, there was another aspect to Matthews's career – an intransigence in his playing style and personality, both of which were questioned by numerous individuals within the game either directly or indirectly. The world of 1950s footballers' autobiographies was one reporting a supposedly nirvana-like existence where 99 per cent of players got along in harmony with one another for 99 per cent of the time, and total deference was shown to all figures of authority. These anodyne documents must be assessed like any historical document with a focus on layers of interpretation.

There is deeper evidence that some players, particularly Billy Wright, thought Matthews a burden, who was achingly predictable in his enclosed and selfish universe, stuck out near that white line. Fundamentally Matthews played exactly the same way and did the same things in 1953 as he did in 1938 and would continue to do so until 1965. According to Nat Lofthouse, Matthews didn't like three things – smoking, swearing and the ball played three yards either side of him, but this comment focussed on just one aspect of the limiting elements of Matthews's overall game. Matthews always insisted that the ball was played directly to feet. He didn't track back, he didn't come back into defence to collect the ball, he didn't tackle, he didn't head the ball and he didn't really score that many goals. In 440 appearances for Blackpool he only scored 18 times. Matthews was a genius at one thing: the perfection of wing play and beating the man wide, driving to the line and cutting back for a cross into the box.

At Wembley in the 6-3 game he stood isolated, waiting and waiting for the ball to be played into his feet, as he did in the 800-plus matches of his professional career. Some days it resulted in the Wizard's wand being waved, leaving dozens of full-backs with twisted blood. Defenders floundering across oceans of mud, uncontrollable, as the factory and mill workers in the crowds pissed themselves laughing at the momentary misfortune of a fellow working man skidding out of play and into the dead zone that surrounds every pitch. Other days it didn't work – through being nailed into oblivion by a size ten working boot with studs nailed into it, or supply being cut. Whether it worked or not, Matthews never changed his game and though he was the dream for many, for others he was expendable. This was the opinion of numerous England selectors between his debut game against Wales in September 1934 and his final match against Denmark in May 1957. Matthews played in 54 of 122 internationals in that time, meaning he appeared in only 44 per cent of England's games.

The passage of Matthews's involvement in the 1950 World Cup epitomised this dichotomy. The Brazilians spent a fortune on the tournament with thousands toiling on the vast construction project of the Maracanã Stadium in Rio de Janeiro. The saucer-shaped mega stadium overtook Hampden Park as the world's largest football-specific venue and accommodated an incredible 200,000-plus for the proxy final of Brazil versus Uruguay in 1950. In contrast to this level of commitment, England's priority decision was to send their most famous and best player – Stanley Matthews – not to Brazil but on a Football Association representative tour of Canada.

In one of the plethora of Matthews autobiographies from his playing days, he used the basis of the 1950 World Cup defeats to attack the approach of Walter Winterbottom. Matthews consistently exhibited a paradoxical double standard to coaching. A man who was obsessed with personal fitness and individual performance, and perfecting his craft, held the counter view that top players couldn't be coached. In *The Stanley Matthews Story* published ten years after the calamitous defeats to the USA and Spain, he summed up his thoughts on the matter, 'You cannot tell the star players how they must play and what they must do when they are on the field in an international match. You must let them play their natural game ... their minds shouldn't be full of now I must do this or that when the ball arrives at their feet.'

In this one brief quote Matthews perfectly summarised the split present in English football between the statics and the adaptors. England just letting a player do what he wanted had worked against Italy in 1934, the 8-0 demolition of Scotland in 1943 and the 10-0 annihilation of Portugal in 1947, so there was absolutely no requirement for interference by the likes of Winterbottom and his attempted application of concepts such as peripheral vision.

Matthews learned the basis of his skills on the streets and spaces of the Potteries, as Puskás had done in Budapest, and the endless chain of super players from George Best in Belfast to Maradona in Buenos Aires. It did not seem to have any importance or relevance for Matthews that even if you took two contemporary players of the highest level, such as himself and Puskás, and one played his own game, intellectually refusing to engage in coaching systems to remain in a playing style of 20 years previously, and the other engaged in development and understanding of space and movement, then even the very top tier could improve performance.

Matthews often exhibited contradictory assessments. In 1960 he stated that he felt the 1950 World Cup looked like a piece of cake for England to win and that even after Brazil defeated Mexico 4-0 in the tournament's opening game he was convinced his team would succeed. By 2000 and his final autobiography, the brilliantly written *The Way it Was*, he'd changed his view completely on the matter. The 1950 World Cup was the crux in an argument of international declinism, not the two defeats to Hungary in 1953 and 1954. Matthews wanted to stay behind in 1950 after England were knocked out to learn from the other countries present. The FA party and players left immediately after the third game versus Spain, but at this point, Stanley was arguing that staff and players needed to remain to expand their knowledge of the game.

Matthews's isolationary and aesthetic personality was deeply connected to his position and outlook on the game, and this reserved and somewhat spiky personality affected his relationships with team-mates at club and international level. The almost vacuous nature of footballer autobiographies from the 1950s have to be mined deeply for a truer perspective of interactions between players. Both Matthews and Billy Wright turned autobiographies into a virtual cottage industry during their playing careers. In Matthews's four autobiographies between 1948 and 1960 he offered several clear criticisms to numerous England figures, but the focus of his ire were Wright and Walter Winterbottom and their unusually close relationship. In *The Stanley Matthews Story* he informed the reader that Billy Wright never inspired him as a captain in the international matches they played together. He clearly considered Wright to be Winterbottom's mouthpiece on the pitch and the implicator of the new ideas being introduced into the game, which Matthews was set solidly against.

The traditional English style, which was not closely defined but presumably at least partially involved getting the ball out wide to a flying winger as much as possible, had to be retained and let the continentals do their own thing and develop their own style. The fluidity of the Hungarian system, whether it was the hybrid child of the 'whirl' or the precursor to the total football of early 1970s Holland and West Germany was, in many senses, redundant for Matthews. The core of the game and the problems the English midfield and defence had to contend with were a thousand miles from Matthews over the invisible line which he dared not cross. Large sections of the game encompassed a non-involvement from the 'ageless wonder' which often reduced his role to that of a bystander.

Was Matthews's annoyance and criticism of Wright simply one of jealousy? In his career Matthews had all the accolades and many of the firsts but his England career was regularly disjointed with gaps of two or three years between appearances. Indeed, the 6-3 game followed his reinstatement to the national side in the October 1953 match against the FIFA XI after a two-and-a-half-year absence stretching from April 1951 versus Scotland, whereas the key to Wright's colossal appearance total was the consistency of his selection and long unbroken runs. Matthews commented that one of the main reasons for this was not ability but Wright's relationship with Winterbottom, something that Matthews did not have and did not want. In Matthews's opinion, while Wright was racking up the caps 'left, right and centre', the Wizard played just once in 1949, twice in 1950, once in 1951 and not at all in 1952.

Matthews combined Winterbottom and the selectors together with no separation of their roles and responsibilities. An avowed anti-coacher for top-class players, Matthews was consistently reluctant to see any important advantage or development that Winterbottom and his emphasis on coaching brought to the national team. Matthews certainly didn't conclude an accurate assessment of the immediate post-Hungary match personnel changes. He stated in *The Way it Was*, 'Our defensive shortcomings were exposed to the full and a few players who were favourites with selectors, I believe primarily because they said the right things before games and at the post-match banquets, were seen not to possess sufficient quality to play at this level ... performances of some players against Hungary did not prevent them going on to win future England caps, one player in particular going on to amass a bountiful supply.' In this one statement Matthews clearly communicated his negative views on the weakness of selectors and Winterbottom, the English defence and midfield and specifically Wright and his 'bountiful supply' of caps. The reality was somewhat different with the defensive personnel post 6-3 and, particularly, post 7-1 being overhauled considerably. Ramsey and Johnston never played for England again after the Wembley defeat and after conceding 30 goals in one season Merrick followed. By the conclusion of the 1954 World Cup in Switzerland there were only two survivors – Wright and Dickinson.

Matthews continued in a negative frame to the selectors and Winterbottom with their decision to stick with the same defence for the opening game of the 1954 World Cup after being annihilated at the Népstadion only a couple of weeks before. He blended the triumvirate of mega-defeats together and concluded that there hadn't been a great deal learned from these losses. Once again this appeared to be in direct contradiction to Matthews's thoughts closer to the actual events when he was wholly negative to a coaching, or as he termed it a 'Europeanised' approach being phased in by Winterbottom. In 1960's *The Stanley Matthews Story*, when Matthews was still an active professional player but at 45 years of age was no longer wearing an England shirt, he exclusively argued for a total return to traditional styles. He described some of Winterbottom's unspecified changes as radical and was clear he did not agree with them. The focus of Matthews's ire was the change in the style of play. The phasing in of a new style of play by Winterbottom was communicated in only negative language – it was a continental style and it had not been successful. Matthews was not having this at all and emphasised that England needed to stick to their own style which brought great success in the past, as it was natural.

The relationship between the man and the player defines and envelops one another. Matthews was a prime example of this interconnectivity. Part of the hagiographic wonder of Matthews was the dichotomy between his physical appearance and the dart and speed with which he destroyed three successive generations of Football League cloggers and smashers whose primary aim was to bounce him into row Z. No matter that the collective analysers from 1932 to 1965 had seen him do it a thousand times before, it still made their pens and typewriters overflow with effusiveness as the slight, little man in the massive, ill-fitting kit shot down the line. Matthews always looked ten years older than he was, more with the appearance of a man who ran a little shop in Burslem than the most famous international player of the pre-television era. The slight frame, slicked-back receding hair, the stooped stance, the gigantic shorts – as if he'd put on the shorts belonging to a man who was 6ft 4in – an absolute fitness fanatic who eschewed smoking and drinking when almost all professional players enjoyed both vices regularly without a care. He purged his body through fasting early in the week. After a match his discipline to his craft was absolute and this pure focus was showcased by his distancing from other players. He was in a team but separate, away from the fulcrum, self-obsessed and highly critical of those not up to his standards or who even acknowledged acclaim. Stan Mortensen wrote how Matthews admonished him once for raising his hand as they were walking off the pitch together and the crowd were chanting his name.

Perhaps the writer who came closest to capturing the Matthews paradox was Arthur Hopcraft, who epitomised the Wizard with his worker's face and frailty. The popularity of Matthews can also be explained in that he fitted a further archetype – that of the sensible, working-class, skilled manual worker who knew his place and always showed deference. The safe worker, no threat, who inhabited a world of church attendance, moderate politics and read self-help books of the Samuel Smiles variety.

Fundamentally, footballers were from the communities that came to watch them. They looked, dressed and thought the same and by and large they remained part of this class during their playing careers and after. The folk hero such as Meredith, Lawton, Finney or Matthews was untouchable in terms of their special skill, but they stayed within the fold as well-paid skilled manual workers. Primarily they occupied this rather unique position due to the restrictions on their earning powers. The other area that bequeathed folk hero status was their behaviour off the pitch, and no one exemplified this more than Matthews. He was never controversial, always focussed on his job and family and always deferred to authority. Matthews was, as we all are, a representative of his age and class, raised among thrift and the ever-looming demon of debt. There was absolutely nothing glamorous about Matthews – a non-smoker, non-drinker and very careful with his money, or as Ernie Taylor put it, the tightest man in football.

Ernie Taylor: the One-Cap Wonder

Four players from flavour of the month Blackpool lined up for England that November 1953 day against Hungary. In terms of profile the fourth of the four was Ernie Taylor, sandwiched between Matthews and Mortensen, a link between Wright to the wing play of Matthews and the barnstorming power play of Mortensen. Every sentence that ever appeared in newspapers and football programmes connected with Taylor always featured one specific word – little. It was inescapable – Little Ernie Taylor. Perhaps his parents did christen him Little Ernie Taylor, and Ernie was his second name. The reason Taylor was always named with this prefix was because he was little. His other football sobriquets were 'Tom Thumb' and the 'Puck of Football', which encapsulated his perceived role on the pitch as a court jester within the game.

The 6-3 match proved to be Ernie's only England appearance. There were two one-cap wonders in this match; George Robb was the other. Robb's case was the easier to explain, though, as Winterbottom didn't want him in the team. The only reason he got a cap was because Tom Finney was injured.

Taylor was 5ft 4in with, incredibly, size four boots, and like all small professional players who were this size his game was based around pure skill. Forceful play and physical presence were clearly not an option. He was an unusual player who developed an idiosyncratic technique in order to survive and flourish in such a physical period of the game. His role at inside-right was that link from the wing-half, front to back and laterally between the centre-forward and the winger. At club level he was renowned for being a quick-witted player who had a delicate touch and a record for scoring vital goals in big matches. This creative link provided George Robledo and Jackie Milburn with plenty of goals at Newcastle United before his substantial move to Blackpool and did similar for the two Stanleys. In his 242 appearances for Blackpool, it was his defence-cutting passes that caused problems for opponents and brought plenty of goals for Mortensen.

Any assessment of Taylor as a player can't be completed on his one and only England performance, but through his club career. His perceived nature was as a joker whose sharp humour matched his quick-witted play. We see the vagaries of the selection committee, only putting Taylor in with

Matthews and Mortensen on that single occasion; England didn't lose the game 6-0 due to being outplayed and out-thought in the central area and defensive positioning only, they lost 6-3. The forward line could, and they did, justifiably point to the fact that they had done their job and scored three international goals against one of, if not the world's premier team. Taylor had his clear and effective role within this aspect of the game. Indeed, of the attacking five in the 6-3 match – Matthews, Taylor, Mortensen, Sewell and Robb – four did not play in the return hammering in Budapest six months later. Apart from Tom Finney naturally returning for Robb, Sewell was the one who escaped the selectors' axe. Taylor and Mortensen never played for England again, being replaced by Peter Harris and Bedford Jezzard, and Stanley Matthews suffered one of his periodic absences from the national team, to be replaced by Ivor Broadis. Matthews fed off accurate passes to feet and that was what Taylor supplied repeatedly.

In terms of the overall historical effectiveness of the forward line that day, the 6-3 defeat was England's 284th full international, and on the previous occasions where they had scored a minimum of three goals, they had only previously lost on three occasions – 5-4 against Scotland in Glasgow in 1880, 5-3 against Wales in Wrexham in 1882 and 4-3 against Spain in Madrid in 1929. Two defeats way back in the mists of time of the early 1880s and, in a reflection of England's first home defeat to a 'foreign' team, their first loss to a foreign team, Spain. In addition, game 284 was the first time England had scored three goals in a home international and lost to anyone.

In terms of pure statistical record, it is logical for the forward line to state that they fulfilled their responsibility in an international against a top team and the issues were fundamentally elsewhere. A logical approach, and consulting the record books did not appear to appeal to the selectors. Of the four players retained for Budapest, apart from Sewell, the goalkeeper kept his place only to be permanently dropped after the World Cup in the summer of 1954 and the other two individuals who were retained – Wright and Dickinson – occupied the zone of discombobulation that Merrick had assessed as he saw it all unravel in front of him.

Taylor's performance in the high-profile, perhaps the most famous, FA Cup Final of them all, the Matthews Final, was crucial for his call-up to the 6-3 game. No other full England cap followed for Taylor, just a B international in March 1956. Many of the one-cap wonders for England took place in near meaningless matches and tours for which anyone would wonder why on earth the FA even bothered. One thinks of the ludicrous 1983 summer tour of Australia under Bobby Robson, which encompassed three full internationals, or the end-of-season four-match tour of Australia, New Zealand and Malaysia under Graham Taylor in 1991. Clubs, off the record, tell their top players not to go on such tours at the end of a long, hard domestic season, which creates a situation where a whole swathe of first-choice players are 'injured'. This inevitably creates space for those not usually considered for the full international team. However, Taylor's singular cap was rather unusual in that it was in such a high-profile match which had been promoted and advertised weeks in advance with a 100,000 sold-out crowd at Wembley.

Matthews was dropped, though later returned for the 1954 World Cup, and Mortensen was permanently gone after scoring 23 goals in 25 internationals. Therefore, the Tangerine attacking triumvirate was admonished and the link man with his clever and intricate play became superfluous to requirements in another example of the selection committee's strange decisions. The club relationship Taylor developed linking play between Matthews, supplying an endless stream of close, accurate passes and Mortensen was only replicated for the international team on this single occasion.

Stanley Mortensen: the Dynamo

Perhaps no one had as many nicknames in English football as Stanley Mortensen. An indicator of the affection fans had for him was his selection of monikers – the 'Mighty Atom', 'Blackpool Bombshell', the 'Electric Eel' and 'Spring-Heeled Jack'. Comments of 'Matthews for centres, Morty for goals' all pointed to one attribute of Mortensen by all writers and journalists – his overpowering dynamism on the pitch. Mortensen acted as the striking spearhead of centre-forward for England in the 6-3 game, scoring their second goal and for a few minutes bringing the score back to 4-2. His usual position in his 25 appearances was at inside-right, where he returned an incredible international scoring rate of 23 goals. Blackpool provided four players for the Hungary match, with Ernie Taylor and Johnston primarily in for their performances in winning the FA Cup six months earlier. The other two players were Matthews, whose pattern in the national team was rather in and out, and Mortensen, who was a rock-solid pick in the international XI of the early 1950s.

Did anyone ever have an international debut for England to match Stanley Mortensen's in Lisbon in 1947? This was the occasion England were invited as guests for the official opening of the Stadium of Light and then proceeded to destroy their hosts 10-0. Mortensen contributed four goals on his debut as his powerful running initiated raid after raid on the Portuguese goal. His goal in the 6-3 game was a classic

Mortensen effort, which the crowds and commentators loved, powering through the middle with his electric pace and finishing with a powerful low drive. Mortensen played football and scored goals with the pure exuberance of a ten-year-old on the local park.

Mortensen had had a near-death experience during World War Two when a Wellington bomber he was in crashed. He was dragged from the wreckage suffering severe head and back injuries and was not expected to survive, let alone take up a career as a professional footballer who would make 354 club appearances and score 222 goals for Blackpool. Perspective was different for many who had lived through combat and near-death experiences while in uniform. Football and other competitive sports were important for those who were fortunate enough to earn their living from kicking, hitting or throwing a ball but for most it had its place. A defeat was sometimes difficult to take but it was just a game and despite Bill Shankly's famous and endlessly quoted saying it wasn't a matter of life and death. Mortensen played a natural form of the game which never encompassed the over-the-top histrionics or weight of the world on your shoulders more preponderant in modern football. Tactics and team shape were not part of his outlook. In his 1949 autobiography entitled *Football is my Game* there was absolutely no mention of tactics at all. Fundamentally, this slim volume was a typical footballer's autobiography of its time – there was nothing even the slightest bit controversial or anything polemical written anywhere. Mortensen's ghostwriter developed his views to be nothing other than a hagiography to major figures of the game at that time, particularly Matthews and Winterbottom. All the players in the 6-3 defeat saw Winterbottom in their own terms – the thinker and tactician.

Alf Ramsey saw Winterbottom as the great educator; Billy Wright, the captain and rock of Winterbottom's time as England manager, saw him as a mentor; Stanley Matthews as a waste of time; and Mortensen saw Winterbottom as someone who made training interesting and fun. Mortensen did not stress any specific tactical talk or coaching that Winterbottom imbued to his players. Before the famous 1947 match versus Portugal, Mortensen stated that England just rolled up their sleeves and got on with it. This was his personal interpretation and general approach to the game – no messing about, let's get stuck in. Perhaps this was the reality for this particular match. This was very early on in Winterbottom's international management career and, perhaps more poignantly, he thought momentarily with the most incredible forward line available of Matthews, Mortensen, Lawton, Mannion and Finney that the coach of coaches wasn't required too much on this one occasion.

One of the few comments that Mortensen directly made of Winterbottom's coaching was to stress that he was there for specific tasks, and that was his strength. He stated that Winterbottom was not there to tell 11 special players picked, by the selection committee, from 3,000 professionals, how to play football, but he could suggest ways and means of playing winning football. Mortensen meant it was not Winterbottom's role to try to improve individual skill levels, but to complement players as a unit. An interesting argument and a valid summation of Winterbottom's approach in the limited time slots available to him, and many other England managers who followed him. Mortensen took a position somewhere in the middle between Stanley Matthews's view that Winterbottom could teach him nothing, and Ramsey who viewed Winterbottom as the oracle about all that was new in the game.

Mortensen's unusual and almost idiosyncratic playing style can be seen in the 6-3 game, more like an amateur's approach. It certainly made an impression on the football writers and commentators of the 1940s and 1950s. Geoffrey Green clearly had great affection for Mortensen the player and responded positively to his unorthodox style. He commented in *Soccer: The World Game* how Mortensen's game was completely different to the accepted pattern, based on instinct and combining a plethora of attributes – swift darting runs, dynamism, pinpoint finishing, always thinking several moves ahead, immense energy and irrepressible spirit, courage, acceleration and an irreproachable standard of behaviour on the pitch. No wonder Mortensen was a favourite with the crowd, in addition to him playing himself into the ground, most notably as far as Green was concerned in an international in 1947 at Highbury, home of Arsenal, in a pulsating 4-2 victory over Sweden. There's no arguing with Green's point that England football fans always loved a player with an outsized heart – take Kevin Keegan or Bryan Robson, for example.

Charles Buchan was another commentator and former top professional player who deeply admired Mortensen, focussing on his powerful, electric sprints cutting through opposing defences. Buchan connected Mortensen to the far-off football past by arguing he was a player comparable with Steve Bloomer. The establishing and recycling of the endless chain of super-players, where you aren't just good in your own right, you deserve to be connected with names from the pantheon. The inhabitants of the god world become instantly even better through the void of time and the rose-tinted glasses, particularly in an era when it was impossible to independently check. Mortensen was connected back through generations of players to Bloomer, but at the same point he was connected forward to the next group of England strikers. God of the north-east Jackie Milburn had modelled his play on the style of Mortensen with his dynamic, fast-paced style and finishing, when he observed him play for Ashington during World War Two.

When the reckless scythe of the selectors fell after the Wembley debacle and half the side lost their heads, never to play for the international team again, there were most certainly two players whose decapitation was completely inexplicable – Ramsey and Mortensen. Mortensen's 23 international goals in 25 games was a scoring rate almost identical to Jimmy Greaves and Gary Lineker after the same amount of appearances. Most of those performances were at inside-right rather than centre-forward. He scored the second of England's three that misty November day with one of his lung-busting runs through defence and a smart shot. He scored in the two internationals before that game, against Argentina and the Rest of Europe. One wonders what on earth the selection committee were looking for from their strikers. Of course, we can never truly know why Mortensen was permanently dropped because the selectors never really explained themselves in public environments such as the press, so all subsequent points are pure speculation. The overall selection process to abandoning a player with an international goalscoring rate of virtually a goal a game was the deeply studied baby with the bathwater approach.

Mortensen was a player who would have gone on forever if he could. He didn't take the route of a top player retiring while still relatively young, as Kevin Keegan did. He followed the path that Matthews and Peter Shilton went down. Until he had to be carried on to the pitch let alone off it, Mortensen carried on playing. His game had been built around his dynamic burst of speed through the middle, so as his pace diminished due to age, his effectiveness did too. Down the divisions he went, bringing his experience and enthusiasm from Blackpool to Hull City and then on to Southport, Bath City and then to Lancaster City until he was over 40, aiming to replicate forever the incomparable feeling of enjoyment and a crescendo of ecstasy from the last low drive into the corner of the goal. As Rob Daniels perfectly summarised in his history of Blackpool FC, Mortensen didn't play football, he revelled in it. His game was based on a passion where he caught fire as the ball came into his vicinity and he needed that fire for as long as was humanly possible.

Atypical of professional footballers in the pre-big or even fair-money era, Mortensen could earn no more from his football employers than his £14 per week in the maximum wage structure of 1953. Other revenue streams had always been available for higher-profile players such as Mortensen. As hundreds of players did both before and after him, he invested in a small local business. Many chose a pub or a sports equipment shop but being based in Blackpool for several years, he chose a fancy goods shop. Football fans from the north on a regulation day trip to the Pleasure Beach would make a beeline for 'Stanley Mortensen – Fancy Goods and Postcards' so they could tell their mates they'd been served by the man himself.

Jackie Sewell: the Boy of Gold

Directly in front of Jimmy Dickinson and the mirror to Little Ernie Taylor was Jackie Sewell of Sheffield Wednesday, another of the forgotten men of the 6-3 defeat, whose voice was smothered by the fame and words of the likes of Matthews, Wright and Ramsey. Sewell was, unusually for an international player, from Cumberland but from an atypical background in one specific context, he was from a mining community in Kells. Indeed, he had that attribute in common with many other British football figures – Jock Stein, Bill Shankly, Jackie Charlton and Billy Meredith – that immediately after leaving school he took up the option from a limited and small world and worked at the local pit, loading and unloading coal tubs. Professional football of the 1940s and '50s was a tough, physical game where the top players were not paid what they deserved but it was far removed from the dangers of being down the mine. If any motivation were required to maximise a skill which could earn an alternative living, then the extreme physical intensity of the face work provided that stimulus.

Sewell's position in the iconography of the history of English football is assured not through his international career, like Billy Wright, but through an achievement over which he held no power or influence – he cost a British record transfer fee when he was transferred from Notts County to Sheffield Wednesday in 1951 for £34,500. It was unusual that Sheffield Wednesday broke the transfer record for a player whose career and reputation was built in the Second Division, where his goal tally was good but not brilliant. His signing certainly looked like a panic measure to hold off relegation, which did not work as Wednesday did go down.

Sewell was worth more than his weight in gold. The strange and almost degrading position of footballers means their innate employment value is decided by current and future employer and placed in the public domain for all the world to assess the accuracy of the value in the eyes of every fan. The record transfer fee has been held in a chain from the instigation of money into the professional game – the first £100, £1,000, £100,000 or £1m player. A peculiar tag and often an undoubted burden. For some players, it was obvious that they cost more money than any other up to that point in time – Trevor Francis, Bryan Robson or Alan Shearer. The other side of the coin is those players transferred for record fees which flabbergast all those who follow the game, and years later remain inexplicable – David Mills and Steve Daley, for example.

The enormous pressure on any human being, walking on to any pitch with every person in the stadium passing judgement on whether you were worth that record fee. Every missed pass, miscontrol, shot wide or miscommunication with your team-mate met with an extra element of frustration and anger because you are the chosen one. You are the one financially worth more than every other professional player who had gone before.

Sewell was in the group of players who found this unique and desperate pressure a difficult one to deal with. Every newspaper, in an echo of every report tagging Ernie Taylor as 'Little', termed Sewell the 'British record transfer fee' to remind the reader that separate and different judgements applied. A performance two percentage points less than the combined talents of Di Stéfano, Pelé, Cruyff, Maradona or Messi could manage would be destroyed through this special criteria. 'All that money and he couldn't finish that' or 'a record fee and he couldn't even beat that full-back' or 'how much we paid for him – useless', all came cascading down from the terraces a thousand times a season, eating into your mind and destroying your confidence as a player. Some managers were astute enough to understand the destabilising effect being the record holder or passing a new threshold might have on a player's psyche. Bill Nicholson insisted that when Jimmy Greaves signed for Tottenham to end his self-defined hell of playing for AC Milan the transfer fee was £99,999, so as not to burden Greaves with the tag of being Britain's first £100,000 player.

In Keith Dixon's biography of Sewell, the striker was open about the stress and the burden that he suffered as Britain's most expensive player. Sewell was not alone in how this periodically unique title affected him. It had previously been a great burden to Bryn Jones when transferred from Wolves to Arsenal in March 1938 for £14,500, and to Eddie Quigley when he moved from Sheffield Wednesday to Preston in December 1949 for £26,500. Sewell felt that he had no one to help him during this process and was exposed by the Notts County directors, who just wanted the money. He was shattered by the transfer saga and received no formal advice. The agentless Sewell ended up receiving a £20 signing-on fee. The whole experience of carrying the record transfer fee appeared to have been traumatic for the young Sewell. He went to Sheffield as he basically did what he was told and did not question authority. He described it in deeply emotive terms over five decades later, as having the cares of the world on his shoulders and his family being upset, feeling like a pawn in a game of chess.

He wasn't a seasoned, experienced international player who'd played 100 games in the top division, which was the usual criteria for a club breaking the record. Sewell had played only in the second and third tiers, in an attack with ex-England legend Tommy Lawton who had dramatically made the drop to the Third Division South. In 1951, when Sheffield Wednesday signed him, he had not actually played for the full international team, making his debut near the end of that year against Northern Ireland. It was, without question, a risky signing by Wednesday. Peter Jeffs commented in *The Golden Age of Football* that Sewell found the price tag difficult to deal with and did not fulfil his potential with the Owls. However, this was surely too much of a jump in conclusion that potential was not fulfilled as it was being judged on playing at a lower level. Sewell was not Gerd Müller, but in 164 league appearances for Sheffield Wednesday he scored 87 goals, and 228 career league goals in total, but it's just that there were the special rules that applied to the record transfer fee holder. In addition, he won the FA Cup with Aston Villa in 1957 and later had another football career playing and coaching in Northern Rhodesia and Zambia.

Author Tony Pawson also concluded that Sewell's lower-league performances did not translate to fulfilment of promise in the First Division. Sewell voiced his own fears and stresses of the tag of record transfer fee. The thoughts of money value appeared to have deeply affected him, 'When I opened the morning papers and found I had cost Wednesday all that money my worries started afresh.' The game was not for fun or professional performance but for worry and stress. 'Am I good enough' and 'If Wednesday had bought a life-size statue of me made of pure gold it would have cost less' were the thoughts that filled the mind of Jackie Sewell in training, at home and walking on to the pitch at 2.55pm on a Saturday.

At representative level Sewell was experienced in matches prevalent in the late 1940s and early 1950s. He played for an FA XI in 1949, in a B international against Holland in February 1949, and went on the 1950 FA tour of Canada and the USA which included a ridiculous 19-1 victory over Saskatoon and the goalfest FA tour of Australia in 1951 with 11-0 and 17-0 victories over Tasmania, 17-0 against Australia and 13-1 over Queensland. Sewell also played for the Football League on four occasions between 1951 and 1954 against the Scottish League and the League of Ireland.

Sewell was not an experienced full international and the 6-3 game was his fifth cap of his overall six cap total.

He commented that he felt the England camp was a happy one in the short timeframe of pre-match preparation, utilising training facilities at Chelsea. Sewell was in the group of England players who stated that they did not know anything about the Hungarians. This confusing picture of communication and preparation continued with, clearly, some team members involved in some discussions with Walter Winterbottom or a certain level of pre-match knowledge available, but others were not aware or not interested in anything about Hungary. In his biography 60 years after the Wembley game, Sewell put across his different views as to why England performed so poorly. A major factor he saw was that the selectors were too impressed with Blackpool winning the FA Cup in the May and picked four of their players. His other main point was like others – that there were just too many changes, particularly from the two previous matches, against Northern Ireland and FIFA in late 1953. Indeed Ufton, Lofthouse, Quixall, Mullen, Rickaby and Hassall were all tried in these two games and did not feature against Hungary. Sewell appeared to have responded in a similar manner to Matthews and Robb by playing his usual club-style game. This was, according to Nat Lofthouse, that of a no-nonsense direct player who moved the ball quickly to centre-forward or winger. Sewell appeared to have a similar approach to both Mortensen and Robb of a forceful, speedy, direct approach and strong striking prowess.

For Sewell, the 7-1 in Budapest was even worse on all fronts and he described it as the low point of his career. Hungary's work in triangles all around the pitch devastated England with Puskás, 'the little pudding with the magic left foot', as Sewell described him, supreme. Preparation in Hungary was so poor that the players had no knowledge of correct fluid intake in the Budapest heat, resulting in Syd Owen becoming so dehydrated that his body went rigid, and he had to be carried off the pitch. In Sewell's memory there was a repetition of the situation recorded in the 6-3 game at half-time. He argued that there was almost no management input around tactics and that the players were left to try and sort out the situation for themselves.

George Robb: the Amateur

The other one-cap wonder in the 6-3 match was George Robb on the left wing. Stanley Matthews, perhaps the first world-renowned player on the right wing, with Robb, a 90-minute international, on the other. One irrefutable fact about Robb is repeated endlessly – he only played in this one match because the great Tom Finney was injured. Indeed, in the original team meeting, Finney was named as the left-winger. Finney's role was to sit in the Wembley press box and observe both the match itself and the other observers.

Robb, drafted in because a genius was unavailable and not even the replacement that Walter Winterbottom wanted, was the last true amateur to play for the full England team and only signed professional forms for Tottenham Hotspur five months before the 6-3 match. Countless contemporary articles were written in magazines on Matthews and Wright, but those on Robb were far more selective – perhaps just the one in the October 1954 edition of *World Sports Magazine*. Here Robb reflected to journalist George Booth on his experiences and conclusions of the 6-3 game. His main point of interest was to assess Puskás as the supreme modern footballer. In contrast to some England colleagues who made fun of Puskás's physique or, like Harry Johnston, rated Puskás behind a host of British players, Robb interestingly saw the bigger picture and aspects of the future. As Puskás himself stated in the 1950s, the modern player and the modern game was all about movement, specifically off the ball to create space and options.

Robb was the only England player who had seen the Hungarians play before, during the 1952 Olympic tournament which the Magyars won comprehensively and, for many, announced their presence on the world football stage. Robb was an impressed observer of the Hungarians in the final against Yugoslavia. Interestingly, given that Robb had previously seen them and that he had several similarities with Winterbottom, his view and opinion of Puskás *et al* was not sought before, or even after the game. Like Winterbottom, Robb's background was as a schoolteacher, and though he taught history and English he was also a qualified physical education teacher, gaining his qualification from Loughborough College. There seemed to be a few connections for Winterbottom to tap into as a resource, but it never appeared to happen in the build-up to the match or at half-time. Perhaps it was as simple a fact as Winterbottom knew Robb would only be involved for this one game, but then again Winterbottom could never really guarantee anything around selection as he was not in control of that process.

Robb's football journey was certainly in contrast to most of his England team-mates who turned professional almost immediately after leaving school with little or no formal educational qualifications and went straight into the unique and isolated world of professional football. Robb was an amateur, the last amateur, who only signed as a professional player for Tottenham aged 27 for £10. Robb had resolutely turned his back on the professional option even when, allegedly, he was asked to name his own terms to sign for an unnamed Italian club, possibly Padua. He also turned down regular offers to sign for Fulham. For several seasons before this he was content with his studies and teaching and playing top-level amateur football for Finchley in the Athenian League, while holding his teaching post at Christ College, a local grammar school.

Booth's article reported that Robb looked at football through the eyes of an amateur, meaning that Robb had a removed position and disliked 'dressing room lawyers, moaners and groaners on the field'. Robb, not being financially dependent on the game, gave him a removed and separate position in the professional world. The insularity of professional players, like the microcosm of many isolated work environments, was circular and stultifying for someone with outside employment, interests and education. In another sense Robb was the removed amateur – seeing skill and beauty as central to the game, in his interpretation of Puskás as the complete modern player and marvelling at the skills of Puskás's famous drag-back goal. It was the hard-bitten and somewhat cynical professional outlook of players such as Ramsey and Johnston who saw Hungarian players as nothing special and, almost inexplicably, the margin of victory as something of a fluke.

Robb certainly drew the poisoned chalice in his one international appearance – covering at very short notice for one of the greatest players ever to pull on an England shirt, against the best team in Europe and playing for a coach who didn't even want him in the team. However, there was one group Robb was very popular with – the pupils of the school he worked at who were given the afternoon off to watch their sports teacher lining up in front of 100,000 spectators against the *Mitteleuropean* supermen. Robb was a highly experienced amateur international who represented England 19 times and the

Great Britain team in the 1952 Olympics in Helsinki and played in two B internationals. His style was no nonsense, no sophistication, a direct winger who went straight for goal and packed a solid shot.

The priority of Robb's teaching career was emphasised by a clause in his contract saying football could not interfere with his job. His decision to finally sign professionally with Tottenham was under the progressive tutelage of Arthur Rowe, a man with coaching experience in central Europe. Rowe's push and run style had been devastating for a short period, leading to Tottenham's title win in 1951. By the 1953/54 season Tottenham's play had become predictable and in the endless competition between new developments and their containment it had fundamentally been countered and dealt with by opponents. English league football may have been primarily based around the WM formation, but not exclusively so. The specialist and almost extreme role of the English winger meant their eternal position was not directly affected by systems and tactical changes in the centre of the pitch. The mantra for wing play remained the same for decades – receive the ball, beat your man by pace or a trick and get the ball into the box for central strikers to score. Robb's one alteration of this endlessly repeated process was to favour a cut inside of the full-back to create a different angle for centring the ball.

Generally isolated in the match, on the opposite wing to Stanley Matthews, Robb was often peripheral to the enduring pressure that Hungary placed England under. The lot of the winger is among the most isolated on any team if there is no ball supply. If it's not coming to you, do you come inside or track back to receive the ball and then you are grossly out of position and not an effective attacking option, or do you keep your specific position and not be able to engage in the passage of play for considerable periods of time? Matthews, the ultimate English winger, had a very average game overall in the 6-3 defeat, so what could realistically be expected of someone drafted in at the last minute to play with individuals he'd never played with before?

Walter Winterbottom was openly and unusually disparaging about Robb's performance. He claimed Robb was lost with the atmosphere and the size of the crowd, and was stunned by playing against the Hungarians and the pattern of the game. Winterbottom turned a focus here on the vagaries of the selection panel. Robb didn't have a poor game given what was an almost total lack of preparation, but he unfortunately appeared to have been a minor pawn in Winterbottom's constant and ongoing stress with the FA selection committee who controlled the national team.

England did not lose to Hungary due to the performance of Robb on the edges of the play down the left. They lost because they were repeatedly overwhelmed in the central part of the pitch where two of Winterbottom's main men, Wright and Dickinson, were positioned. Robb had flitted into this match, and he flitted out even quicker as he never played for England at full level again, but then neither did Ramsey, Mortensen, Johnston, Eckersley or Taylor. The man he replaced for 90 minutes, Tom Finney, was not as critical of Robb as Winterbottom and saw the forward line as having done their job by scoring three goals. He identified the issues as lying in defence.

Walter Winterbottom: the Boffin

The single most important individual in the development of coaching and introducing change in English football from the late 1940s onwards was, without question, Walter Winterbottom. In the *Oxford Dictionary of Word Origins*

Julia Cresswell informed us that the word 'boffin' was first introduced during World War Two as slang for an older officer, and first appeared in 1945 in *The Times* to denote a scientist or someone engaged in technical research. If we had a football-specific edition there is no doubt that the first recorded entry for boffin would be related to Winterbottom and appear around 1947.

Winterbottom was THE football boffin during the latter 1940s and 1950s as he was literally the only one. Brian Glanville thought he looked like a Corinthian, with works by Xenophon and Homer on his bookshelves. A man whose outlook and approach polarised players into two very distinct camps – those who thought his approach was a total waste of time and those who saw him as a visionary. Of all the players he managed and coached from 1946 to the early 1960s there was almost no one who remained ambivalent to Winterbottom and his ideas.

The two most important decisions of the Football Association in the immediate post-World War Two period were rejoining FIFA and the appointment of Winterbottom to his dual roles as head of coaching and international team manager. There was no question in Winterbottom's mind which of these two jobs was the more important, and that was the position as head of coaching. Both positions were new, and Winterbottom faced negativity from all sides as he tried to implement change to a system that had not fundamentally changed for decades. All innovators face ridicule and tension from those who feel no change or adaptation is necessary and Winterbottom was no different. However, it was Stanley Rous who saw Winterbottom as the future, as an impressive presence, an engaging personality and having a youthful zest. He was a different and new type of figure in football who had several sides to his experience and knowledge –

as a player, a teacher, a manager and an administrator, but above all a professional – and was serious about his role and engaged in deep preparation.

When Winterbottom arrived in his roles in 1946, he found a football system which had been fundamentally stagnant for many years. He voiced the obvious frustrations in 1946 – there was a distinct lack of regular ball practice and a focus on so-termed stamina training based around monotonous laps of the pitch. Many professionals kept their skills secret and perhaps most damning of all was a fairly minimal knowledge of the rules of the game by players. It was from this ground zero point that Winterbottom began to very slowly turn around the super tanker that was English professional football. In addition to this was the outright and obvious hostility from specific groups within the game – some of the established players in the international team, the FA international selection committee and the chairmen of Football League clubs.

The stunning galaxy of players whom Winterbottom held when he took over his national manager's position was, perhaps, the greatest England ever had – Frank Swift, Neil Franklin, Tom Finney, Stanley Matthews, Raich Carter, Tommy Lawton and Billy Wright were all available in 1946 and had all played together in the unofficial wartime internationals. The contempt that some of this group of players had for Winterbottom and his coaching and skills development was open and obvious. Among the main anti-coaching group were Matthews, Lawton and Carter. All three had been professionals since before World War Two and their background, like those of many other players, was that the role of the club manager was a very different one from that which Winterbottom wanted to instil. The prewar football manager did not generally involve himself in day-today training with players but was often a more office-based individual who attended to administration.

The players and club trainer basically just got on with the same fitness and stamina routines week after week, season after season. The most vocal anti-Winterbottom and anti-coaching player, certainly, over time, was Stanley Matthews. In his 1960 autobiography *The Stanley Matthews Story*, he was adamant that Winterbottom had taken the English national team down completely the wrong route. It was Winterbottom who was to blame for England trying to copy continental teams when the focus for the national team should have been 'sticking to the style that brought us great success in the past – which is our natural style!'

There are multiple problems with this overarching statement. Matthews didn't expand on what he meant by either great success or the past. He must have meant pre-World War Two, but England didn't compete fully in the global football environment of this period. Before 1939 England did not compete in any of the first three World Cups of 1930, 1934 and 1938 and had never faced the powerhouse trio of South American football – Uruguay, Brazil and Argentina. In fact, up to 1939 England had only played continental European opposition on 53 occasions and had rigorously stuck to the format of three internationals every year, against Scotland, Wales and Ireland or Northern Ireland. There had been some magnificent displays and impressive victories, such as the 6-3 win over Germany in Berlin in 1938 or the 3-2 beating of world champions Italy at Highbury in 1934. However, to compare the globalising football world that Winterbottom was involved in introducing to England with the interwar period when England were not even a member of FIFA is impossible to assess accurately.

The Boffin Walter Winterbottom, newly appointed to national roles in 1947

Gil Merrick in his Birmingham City jersey which could be from any year between 1930 and 1958

Alf Ramsey in a glamorous early 1950s England photo shoot in someone's back garden

Harry Johnston and Stanley Matthews looking pensive in pre-match line up v Hungary

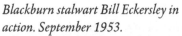

Jimmy Dickinson in his beloved Portsmouth shirt. August 1960

Blackburn stalwart Bill Eckersley in action. September 1953.

*Billy Wright in his
England blazer
holding his 1952
Footballer of the
Year Award*

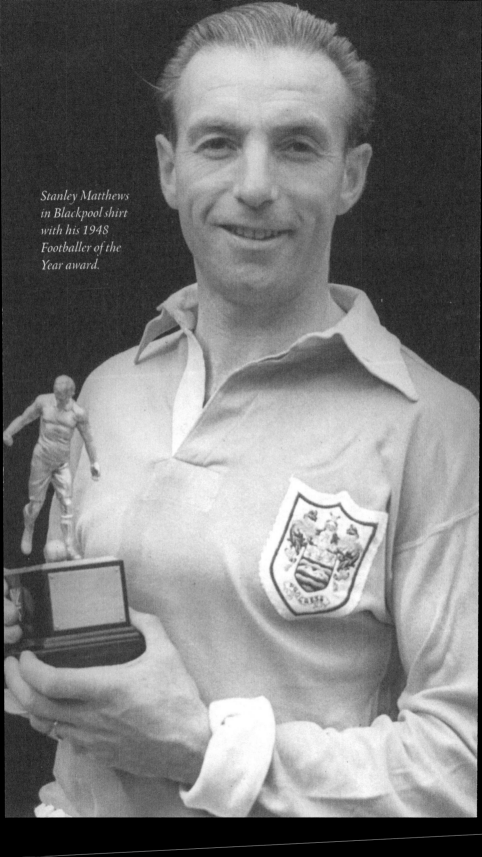

*Stanley Matthews
in Blackpool shirt
with his 1948
Footballer of the
Year award.*

Indisputably Little Ernie Taylor alongside Sam Crowther after signing for Manchester United in 1958

A young, happy Morty wearing the classic velvet England cap

Jackie Sewell in the same back garden pose as Ramsey

George Robb – the last real amateur to play for England, replete in his Tottenham shirt.

Stanley Rous – the FA patriarch with standard issue bowler hat and clipped moustache in 1934

Puskas's belly appears to have vanished during the walk on to Wembley pitch.

Wright and Puskas lead out their club sides in the highly anticipated Wolves v Honved match

Matthews was openly antagonistic to Winterbottom in his public pronouncements as a staunch anti-coacher, stating on more than one occasion that it was just not possible to coach international players and they (by which he included himself) should be left to just get on with their natural game. Matthews's position couldn't be more diametrically opposed to that of Gusztáv Sebes or Béla Guttmann. It seems a decidedly strange conclusion to come from someone who after he retired spent decades travelling to different parts of the globe fundamentally coaching young players.

There was an undoubted distance between Winterbottom and at least some of the players. This was often because they interpreted Winterbottom as different and posh. Winterbottom was a self-improver but his background in Werneth, Oldham, was most certainly not one of privilege. In the class-ridden times of mid-20th century Britain the identifiers of class were much more obvious and rigorously applied than in the early 21st century. Winterbottom certainly didn't eschew the blatant indicators of male, northern, working-class culture, but this is where he started from. His background was one of positional improvement gained through educational achievement. He was a teacher at different levels before being taken under the wing of Stanley Rous and was keen to exude this role in his physical appearance and manners. His horn-rimmed, studious glasses were often commented on but what were you to do if you needed to wear spectacles in 1947 and there were only about three styles to choose from? An important part of his public ensemble was his forever-present smoking pipe, but this was a tool often utilised by relatively young men in responsible employment positions to make themselves look more mature and to be taken seriously. Perhaps this was part of a subconscious process where Winterbottom held his

national management position over men who were only a few
years younger than him. Stanley Matthews, for example, was
only two years younger than Winterbottom.

Perhaps Winterbottom went too far with his attempts
to be seen as a serious leader. In a zeitgeist term for the early
1950s Billy Wright stated that Winterbottom resembled an
atomic scientist. It was clearly this dichotomy that though
Wright saw his national manager taking the team forward in
the nuclear age with diagrams, plans and concepts many of
the immediate postwar team saw Winterbottom as Tommy
Lawton did – 'that bloody PE teacher'.

In terms of the gap between Winterbottom and the
players, the major crime on his behalf wasn't his education
or wartime service in the RAF but the perception, by many,
that he'd never been a player himself and, therefore, couldn't
possibly know what on earth he was talking about. A trope of
the game, certainly in Britain, has always been that you can't
'know' the game unless you were a top professional player
yourself and that the true manager and coach can only really
understand football and communicate that understanding if
they had been a professional at the higher levels for hundreds
of games and probably an international too. Even in the
modern era of Arsène Wenger, José Mourinho and Rafael
Benítez, none of whom were top players or in the cases of
Benítez or Mourinho professionals, this opinion still crops
up but in previous decades it was an unshakeable foundation
of football belief in Britain.

There was an inestimable connection between being a
successful professional player and a successful professional
manager. In a sense it was a self-fulfilling prophecy as if
only former top players got the management jobs in the first
place then clearly only they could succeed. The mirror of
success and failure down the decades is clear. The list of

successful managers who were top players is long – Matt Busby, Bill Shankly, Stan Cullis, Bill Nicholson, Joe Mercer, Brian Clough, Don Revie and Alf Ramsey – but so is their opposite list of former top players who fundamentally failed in management, including Matthews, Bobby Moore, Bobby Charlton, Billy Wright and Peter Shilton. The position of exclusion to coaches and managers with no pedigree in England reached a position of *reductio ad absurdum* in the situation of George Raynor, the former Sweden national manager, who guided the team to the 1958 World Cup Final but almost laughably could only find employment in England as manager of Skegness Town.

The players were certainly not the only group who saw Winterbottom's role and ideas as pointless, if not ridiculous. The other two groups who, fundamentally, were negative on Winterbottom's double role were the councillors of the FA and league club chairmen. All these powerful actors taking a position of exclusion emphasises the incredible achievement of Winterbottom to get anything done on the coaching front in a national context. These two groups had more impact on the parameters of what Winterbottom saw as his second job, national manager; the position that he always focussed on as primary was as national director of coaching. This colossal responsibility of establishing a new national coaching structure was what truly motivated Winterbottom. He knew, realistically, that he was never going to convert the likes of Matthews and Tommy Lawton to his model and the role of coaching, but Winterbottom was in it for the long run.

The development of a genuine national coaching structure would, clearly, take some considerable time, but during progress there would be a phasing out of the old guard of anti-coachers who would be replaced by a new group of players more appreciative of Winterbottom and his coaching. There were players in the 6-3 team who were fellow passengers with Winterbottom in their appreciation of what he was trying to do – Ramsey, Mortensen and Billy Wright for certain. This position of some in the team being pro-coaching and tactics and those clearly negative or perhaps neutral, has led, partly, to a very confusing interpretation of Walter Winterbottom's role and input to match preparation and in such crucial areas as a response and analysis at half-time in the 6-3 match. Stan Mortensen, at least in the public arena of his 1949 autobiography *Football is My Game*, stressed at considerable length that though the team was picked for Winterbottom, it was well worth having him as a manager for, at least, three specific attributes – planning moves for goals, preparation in assessing opponents and creative training sessions which were not as monotonous as at club level.

Membership of FIFA and Winterbottom's coaching programmes were two of the key developments by which those who perceived the gap, such as Rous, tried to close it. One of the major avenues for Winterbottom of coaching development was through the establishment and running of the FA coaching badges aimed at professional players with a more progressive outlook. Author Brian Scovell wrote that this was Winterbottom's greatest achievement, to lift English professional players from their isolation, both in terms of ideas and physical contests. The list of players who attended the earlier Winterbottom-led FA coaching courses in the late 1940s and 1950s is a veritable who's who of individuals who became important coaches and managers themselves in the following 30 years – Don Howe, Bill Nicholson, Malcolm Allison, Jimmy Hill, Ron Greenwood and Bobby Robson.

Winterbottom had an important and immediate effect on the outlook of this group of players, and many others who dispersed his ideas out to clubs when devotees returned to their weekly routines. For those who were open to new ideas and approaches, Winterbottom was the lightning rod and his clear communication skills were crucial to getting people on board. Don Howe and Alf Ramsey were certainly two early admirers of Winterbottom. Howe praised Winterbottom's approach to focus on mental preparation for games and his knowledge of developments in the world game with reference to the Brazilians and their fastidious preparation. Ramsey also enjoyed Winterbottom's long, directive conversations where he encouraged views and opinions from players in a discussion rather than a lecture. Tom Finney also emphasised that Winterbottom's forte was coaching and blending individual skills for a common aim. A further acolyte of Winterbottom's was Bobby Robson, who started to attend the FA coaching courses after he was a spectator at the 6-3 game. He and some of his Fulham team-mates, Jimmy Hill, Ron Greenwood and Jackie Goodwin, found in Winterbottom a like-minded outlook at changing and improving the game.

A key component for Winterbottom in the development of coaching was the lack of interference and curtailment that he experienced in comparison to the national team. Fundamentally there was no selection committee in the development of coaching structures. Rous was keen for Winterbottom to push the case and funding of a national coaching programme, including the utilisation of Lilleshall for residential courses. One of the major avenues by which Winterbottom distributed his coaching philosophy was through his successful book, *Know the Game*, and in other prominent articles such as those present in the *FA Book for Boys*, which was published annually by Naldrett Press. This was a popular and respected publication with content standard above that of most boys' annuals.

In the 1954 edition of the *FA Book for Boys*, Winterbottom wrote a central article aimed at the intelligent schoolboy player which explained the overall complexity of the square ball or pass. Winterbottom focussed on one of his hobby horses, peripheral vision, explaining it in pedagogical terms. He stressed to boys how the top players would 'split their glance' between the ball at their feet and other players around the individual in possession. The other skill stressed in this article was movement off the ball, particularly when your team was not in possession. The article was accompanied by some in-depth diagrams to reinforce the importance of these concepts to quality play. Winterbottom made a fascinating point for boys to appreciate movement and positioning by focussing on one player in a match and just watching him and what he did. This might seem like an obvious thing to do from a point of coaching, developing an understanding of the game, but at its core level it's a very unnatural way in which to watch a game, by actually not watching it at all. The international players may well have scoffed at ideas such as this, but Winterbottom was laying the groundwork for future players and coaches at all levels of the game with these important points.

Winterbottom was deeply involved in the content of the *FA Book for Boys* for numerous years and though other articles in the 1953/54 edition were not directly attributed to him they certainly had his stamp on them. These included the introduction of themes such as tactical preparation and pre-match meetings to discuss an opponent's strengths and weaknesses and a four-phase training module with transitional, foundation, form-building and form-sustaining periods. One can appreciate why there was a reluctance to accept Winterbottom's ideas and processes by several players, particularly in the late 1940s and 1950s.

Winterbottom had two powerful and special relationships in the first decade of his time as England manager – Stanley Rous and Billy Wright. Rous was more responsible than anyone for Winterbottom gaining and sustaining his position. Wright was Winterbottom's premier captain and played more times for England under the manager than anyone else. The only other relationship between coach and captain that got close to replicating this one was in the 1980s between the two Robsons, Bobby and Bryan.

Wright and Winterbottom was an unusual relationship as Wright formed the role of *aide-de-camp*, bridging a very wide gap between the approach of club and international managers. Stan Cullis at Wolverhampton Wanderers and Winterbottom had fundamentally opposed views on most football-related issues. Cullis was most certainly not a fan of radical introductions or 'funny ideas', as he termed them. He never seemed to have been specific over what he meant by this, but it's not hard to see that Winterbottom's development of peripheral vision and tiered training programmes would have been on the Cullis funny ideas hit list. It's not that the powerful in English football were not enthusiastic about coaching as an isolated issue, they were not enthusiastic and indeed negative about almost any change to the game which altered the sport away from a perceived Golden Age. Football being played on a Sunday, the World Cup, floodlit matches and European competitions were all seen as unnecessary developments that would sully and diminish the established nirvana.

Soccer Partnership is an unusual book in the history of English football, written by the journalist Bob Ferrier.

With input from Winterbottom and Wright it assessed their relationship, which was the core one between the manager and a player throughout the 1950s. Ferrier came to some strange conclusions. Paramount among these was his view that when Winterbottom took over as England manager the senior players enthusiastically embraced his new approach and increase in coaching. As previously outlined, this is fundamentally nonsense with Matthews, Tommy Lawton and Wilf Mannion all negative to basically any form of coaching at all. The idea that if any of these players were to be coached or guided it might have made them just five per cent better or given an appreciation of team over individual performance was not present. Even someone as anti-funny ideas as Cullis appeared to be able to see the advantages of introducing coaching to a young Stanley Matthews.

Cullis saw Matthews as too individualistic, as did Wright, and the Wolves manager mused on work or 'coaching' he would instil in a young Matthews: 'If a young Matthews came to Molineux tomorrow, I would endeavour to use his tremendous skill to a greater effect than perhaps it has been used in the past. With his speed, superlative ball control, ability to slip easily past a defender and accurate shot, Matthews should surely have scored many more goals than he has done.' The core of Cullis's point is clear: Matthews was an incredible player but with his guidance he could have been even better and contributed more to the team. In the core of the matter all coaching is guidance. That's if Matthews had listened, of course. Indeed, Matthews was a consistent critic of Winterbottom, coaching and the England setup, so much so that he was given a slapped wrist by the FA in 1952 for such criticisms in a newspaper article.

There remained an anti-Winterbottom position for many years after he took control. A decade down the line there were still some players who questioned the value of his approach. A young Bobby Charlton was one who saw Winterbottom's impact as limited, due to issues with communication. In a somewhat contradictory conclusion to players such as Wright or Ramsey, Charlton stated that talking to players was a weakness of Winterbottom's. This was due to his opinion that Winterbottom had never really been a professional player. Charlton expanded this point to say that he meant Winterbottom had not been a professional player to the same level as Matt Busby or Cullis. This was true in that Winterbottom was never an international, but it does a disservice as he had most certainly been a professional.

The camps of pro- or anti-Winterbottom could be rigid, and the most pro-Winterbottom voice in the 6-3 team most definitely belonged to Billy Wright. In three of his multifarious autobiographies – *Captain of England*, *Football is My Passport* and *One Hundred Caps and All That*, Wright spoke about Winterbottom in exhaustive detail. From the beginning of their long-standing professional relationship Wright was keen to project Winterbottom in the most hagiographical of terms. Wright carefully developed his public image over his years at the top of the game and rarely criticised anyone in public, partly to avoid unnecessary negative press himself and jeopardise his position as England's captain. In the era of the maximum wage Wright was one of few players who earned a very good living from the game, which was clearly built around his high profile as captain for over a decade.

Certainly, in *Captain of England* from 1950 Wright took a position of 100 per cent positive points about Winterbottom. In a close working relationship with someone over a decade-long period, who would agree with their line manager and feel their manager made the correct decision every single time? The truth is it never happens. This dichotomy was the crux of Winterbottom's career as England manager and specifically the 6-3 game. What was his effectiveness in areas such as match preparation, tactics and half-time motivation? There was a picture of confusion around these critical issues, not just of their effectiveness, but whether they even took place. Wright put forward an immediate and interesting proviso regarding tactics in *Captain of England*, which was a valid point, 'Too many folks expect tactical talks will automatically bring success, but Winterbottom, from the beginning of our association, never allowed us to forget that 11 opponents are not going to stand still and watch plans develop for defeating them.'

Despite this almost counter-intuitive statement Wright argued that preparation and tactical analysis, both pre- and post-match, were particular strengths of Winterbottom. This was, according to Wright, a fully inclusive process with players invited to bring forward their opinions in an open discussion. Winterbottom would offer his analysis of opponents in pre-match talks which were a consistent and popular feature of the pre-international get-togethers. He appeared to have made these an inclusive exercise by inviting players to contribute. Presumably some, such as Ramsey, contributed at length but once Matthews had stated his *reductio ad absurdum* point what more was there to say? Half-time team talks were, according to Wright, regularly inspiring and often turned around a level of performance.

Winterbottom's preparation for the 6-3 game appeared to have been to a level not followed before. Winterbottom, accompanied by a coterie of the press, flew to Budapest to watch Hungary's international against Sweden, which ended 2-2. Winterbottom concluded that Hungary were good enough to beat any team in the world – except Sweden, presumably. It was after this match that Winterbottom told

Wright that England would adopt the 'retreating defence' when they hosted Hungary in November. Admittedly writing nine years later, Wright was clear that defensive duties and approach had been discussed by Winterbottom with responsible players before the game and the result was the adoption of this specific system. A simplistic approach, this defensive system was exactly as the name suggested, as the defence held off the man in possession until the optimum moment for a challenge, rather than independent challenges further up the field. Of course, as in any collective system, it could only be effective if all elements were working cohesively. If one individual with defensive responsibilities did not move into the allocated space or hold a unit line with everyone, then space was created.

Wright was, fundamentally, a voice for Winterbottom, stressing the issues that restricted his approach and the implementation of his ideas. The resistance of numerous individuals to coaching and tactics, though these individuals were not named, and the consistent lack of preparation time were two vital points where the impact of Winterbottom's work was heavily restricted. The game that Wright stated was the epitome for a lack of preparation was the return match in Budapest and the devastating 7-1 defeat. The lack of practice training sessions extenuated the fundamental problem of blending 11 club players, often not Winterbottom's preferred choices, with their own specific styles into a smooth, co-ordinated unit in a couple of days.

The post-match was often as challenging as the pre-match, at home internationals, as there was not the facility to carry out analysis due to players leaving immediately. The fallacy of a football revolution being initiated 16 minutes after the referee Leo Horn blew the final whistle on the 6-3 match was encapsulated in that statement. No doubt Wright's analysis of the English setup could have been written at many points subsequently, for example during Bobby Robson's time as manager between 1982 and 1990. The only occasions that the players spent time together over longer periods was on the touring parties. On tours Winterbottom and the players had an opportunity to spend time living, talking and practising together as a genuine team.

Though Wright was clear that there had been specific pre-match preparation of the retreating defence, the actions and views of other players question whether this was the case. Most notable was the example of Harry Johnston, who appeared to have been more focussed on picking up the man with the ball, Hidegkuti, rather than forming a retreated defensive position. Hidegkuti roamed around in this available space with the England defence playing deeper, creating opportunities. Johnston appeared intent on marking Hidegkuti as he was holding the ball behind Puskás and Kocsis. Did Johnston not listen to Winterbottom's tactical discussion? Was he at the meeting? How can two men standing ten metres or so apart, as in Wright and Johnston, have had such diametrically opposed views of the tactical roles they should have taken up?

Bobby Charlton, though playing later, was another who did not see Winterbottom as a clear communicator of a tactical approach. He insisted that before matches there was no tactical planning at all and that Winterbottom would just focus on individuals and not as a team or what system they played. In absolute contradiction to the position Wright held that tactical discussion was a permanent fixture of pre-match planning, Charlton was adamant, 'I cannot remember one single occasion on which Winterbottom said how England were to play tactically.' Two of England's greatest players, the first two to play 100 internationals, had totally different positions on whether Winterbottom brought a tactical awareness to the international team or not. Stanley Matthews was also clear that though Winterbottom had recently seen Hungary play against Sweden there was no mention of how England were to counteract the positioning of Hidegkuti. Though given Sir Stanley's aversion to any form of coaching or instructions, it seemed rather odd for him to comment on this issue in a negative context.

Another listener and talker of the game, Alf Ramsey, was of the view that tactics were a clear part of Winterbottom's pre-match analysis. He categorically stated in his 1952 Stanley Paul autobiography *Talking Football*, 'Tactical talks by Winterbottom proved what a great judge he is of a football team, in an easy-to-understand style.' The listeners listened and the non-listeners didn't hear anything. Further, according to Ramsey, was a confirmation of Wright's view that Winterbottom was a splendid and skilful speaker, who contrived to blend together the players' ideas and to pick out chinks in the opponents' armour and suggest ways and means of taking advantage of them – tactics. Though this rather slim book was published before the 6-3 game it communicated a process that, as far as Ramsey was concerned, took place on a consistent basis.

Stan Mortensen in *Football is My Game* concluded that one of the advantages of having Winterbottom as a team manager was that he always looked at international teams beforehand and informed his players of opponents' strengths and weaknesses. A focus was given to weaknesses so that the England team could go into a match with a clear attacking plan designed to maximise impact on to the perceived weaknesses. Mortensen's book was published in 1949 in the early stages of Winterbottom's role as international manager, and the need or requirement for this post was still perceived as a novelty and questioned by many within the game.

Tom Finney would have played in the 6-3 defeat but for injury, though he was still inside Wembley that day and 50 years later in his 2003 autobiography he stressed that one of Winterbottom's great strengths within the game was that 'he was known as a supreme judge of opposition teams'.

Confusion still reigns as to the complex impact of Winterbottom in his tactical awareness and how this was communicated to his players.

Stanley Rous: the Patriarch

Stanley Rous was the individual who bestrode the old and the newer football worlds that England moved to at glacial speed. His extraordinary administrative career involved decades at the peak of the game. He was, domestically and internationally, secretary of the FA and then secretary-general of FIFA from 1934 to 1974, when his career at the top was ended by the *realpolitik* manoeuvring of Joao Havelange. Forty years of meetings with the powerful, debates, missives, reports, recommendations and minutes all focussed on both the day-to-day and strategic functioning of the game. Rous knew everyone and everyone had some form of contact with him. The changers and revolutionaries whispered in one ear, while the traditionalists held him by the arm.

Rous bridged eras in the game from the spectacularly pompous and arrogant Sir Frederick Wall, who wore full top hat and tails to England internationals, through to shaking hands with self-declared Maoist sympathiser Paul Breitner during the 1974 World Cup in West Germany. As Brian Glanville, a man who did not like Rous on a personal basis, argued, you could criticise the social climbing, autocratic ways, snobbery and his clear indifference to the players themselves but Rous was clearly a force for the progress of the game which he initiated both in the domestic and international arenas.

This was the core of Rous, a man who combined both the old and the new, with a public persona that fundamentally mimicked the ways of the FA committee brethren of the interwar period, but in his deeds and actions he was crucial in the slow-moving, modernising process of the English and British game. Rous was never a player, coach or manager – he was a schoolmaster and a referee. These positions shaped his outlook on the game. Rous's earlier life was based around his employment as a master at Watford Grammar School. In 1927 he was appointed a Football League referee and it was there that he developed his own system for officiating a match more effectively. This was a diagonal system running back and on to a 45-degree axis to give a deeper dimensional understanding of live action and encompassing differing angles to view foul play and offsides. Rous rose to the pinnacle of the refereeing world and in one extraordinary week during which he found time to apply for the post at the Football Association he also refereed the Welsh FA Cup Final on a Thursday, then the FA Cup Final on the Saturday, and then the day after that he made his way over to Antwerp to take charge of an international. Despite these pressures on his time, his application to replace Sir Frederick Wall at the FA was successful. Rous held this incredibly powerful and influential post from 1934 to 1961 before moving over to the ultimate international post at FIFA.

To read the minutes of the board meetings of the Football Association is an overwhelmingly dry experience to the point of inducing tears, but it's a pure indicator of the footballing responsibilities of the FA and Rous specifically. These included schools, amateur, FA Cup, coaching, lectures, disciplinary committee, the match and grounds committee, publication committee, youth, benevolent fund and finances. In his rather slim memoir from 1978 *Football Worlds: A Lifetime in Sport*, Rous focussed on the broad range of changes he was central in introducing during his long time as FA secretary – improvements to playing kit, floodlighting, training get-togethers for players, national courses for groundsmen, managers and schoolboys, coaching qualifications, publications of textbooks, annuals, diaries and FA news and the use and development of television in promoting football. An incredibly exhaustive list.

A core part of Rous's work and influence was through *The Post War Memorandum*. Rous considered the future development of football in England during the war and drew up his memorandum to consider the future pattern of the game over the next quarter of a century. This wide-reaching document covered almost all aspects of the game and was to have a far-reaching effect in the next three decades. The memorandum focused on county youth tournaments, under-23 international competitions, urged all four British associations as soon as possible to rejoin FIFA, and specialist courses for referees, players, coaches, managers, trainers and administrators. Here was the ground zero in the tensions between the modernisers and the remainers.

Opportunities for development in the game formally and nationally started with this work of Rous and, crucially, Winterbottom. However, this produced a bigger split in football than had existed previously, with those who wished to learn and develop taking up these new options, and those who felt that coaching and such concepts as peripheral vision had nothing to offer, clearly not being involved in any of the Rous programme. Two separate worlds developed and re-enhanced themselves based on two fundamental opposing outlooks: those who embraced coaching and developments involving ideas from continental Europe and those who believed that the English and British game was the best and that the focus needed to be the retention and promotion of the previously successful aspects which had brought perceived success. This is the split that further manifested itself during and after the 6-3 game.

A central part of Rous's post-World War Two programme was, indisputably, coaching. He argued that maybe for a small number of natural geniuses such as Stanley Matthews or Jimmy Greaves coaching might not be relevant, but these players were the exception. For the overall development and maintenance of the professional game and the tens of thousands of amateur players, coaching was crucial. However, the paradoxical pattern of the interwar period continued in terms of the relevance of coaching in England. One of the most successful and influential pre-World War Two coaches, Jimmy Hogan, among his myriad of appointments, was the instructor at the first FA coaching course in 1936. Though Rous was no fan of Hogan, he had set a ball in motion with Hogan's interwar disciples including Alex James, Arthur Rowe and specifically the individual with incomparable influence on the development of coaching in England – Walter Winterbottom.

The split between the moderns and the remainers in their battle for football was no clearer than in the employment journey of those who attended FA coaching courses. Many found employment in England very difficult to obtain so Rous utilised his power and influence to find postings across the world. In a complimentary approach to the height of imperialism, Rous acted in the highest manner of a minister at the India Office dispatching civil servants to maintain the Raj. The result of this bizarre scenario was that coaching in many areas of the world improved dramatically whereas the coaching void within England continued and the promotion of old pros and old techniques dominated. Therefore, the discussions at numerous clubs continued in the same pattern as prewar.

International coaching posts were just one aspect of Rous's global outlook, which ultimately led to him becoming president of FIFA in 1961. It was a journey of considerable outlook change for the FA from when Rous became the paramount force. His predecessor at the FA was the avowed xenophobe Sir Frederick Wall, a man who in his autobiography *50 Years of Football* focused on the halcyon days of the game as taking place in the pre-professional era of the 1860s and 1870s when standard codification came into being. Wall turned down the opportunity to join FIFA at its inception in 1904 with all the implied arrogance of an Ottoman emperor deigning to listen to an unknown provincial satrap.

Though Rous had been involved in an internationalist approach before World War Two – particularly the organising of FA tours to continental Europe and the infamous Nazi salute by the England team in Berlin in 1938 – it was really after World War Two that his influence began to nudge the colossal glacier on a different path. His absolute base for FA incompetence was three years prior to the 6-3 game, in Brazil and the debacle of the 1950 World Cup. He tried to intervene in getting Matthews off the FA Canada tour and down to Brazil ready to face the USA, whom Rous regarded as no pushovers. The absolute calamity of that result only exemplified for Rous the total stupidity of having the team manager divorced from the selection process. He wanted to initiate a structure where the key was meritocracy.

This meritocracy was to be achieved through a seemingly endless range of changes and improvements Rous made to the game – apart from his avowed belief in training he introduced training programmes using filmed techniques, promoting football at youth level for school leavers, he appointed a press officer and a public relations officer at the FA to improve newspaper coverage and was involved in the introduction of the Inter-Cities Fairs Cup. All these areas were introduced by Rous directly or by people he put in place. Paramount in these Rous-led developments in the immediate postwar period was the rejoining of all four of the British associations to FIFA.

Those Who Saw the 6-3

THE GENERAL interest in the Hungary international at Wembley was absolute. Wembley acted as a gigantic north London magnet drawing in all those interested in the game and seeing the best. Perhaps, surprisingly, this was only the second truly foreign team that had played a full international at Wembley, after Argentina in 1951. The number of individuals, in addition to those who were directly involved, who watched from the terraces and later had a significant impact on the British club game and English international side is quite astounding. Purely in terms of future England managers there was Alf Ramsey at full-back and both Ron Greenwood and Bobby Robson, professional players in 1953, keen observers from the terraces. It's unclear whether the other permanent England manager between 1963 and 1990 – Don Revie – was at the game, but he was an acknowledged admirer of the Hungarians throughout his managerial career.

They came from far and wide to experience the Magyars and see Puskás *et al* in the flesh. Glasgow Celtic sent down their first team to watch England against the FIFA Select XI and Hungary in late 1953. Bob Kelly at Celtic, as a reward for a highly successful 1953/54 season, subsequently sent the whole playing staff to the 1954 World Cup to broaden their football education. Among the Celtic players was Jock Stein, as Archie Macpherson stated in his biography of Stein, 'Puskás and company put a gleam in Stein's eye and an idea in his sights that stirred his imagination, and that in itself was to rub off on anyone who put on boots for him at any stage.' Also, from further afield came future Real Madrid superstar and team-mate of Puskás, Raymond Kopa. He attended the self-styled 'Match of the Century', paying for the trip to London with the bonus he had received for winning the French league with Stade de Reims.

Ron Greenwood was most certainly at the 6-3 game to try and learn everything he could about the Hungarians and observe how football had developed on the continent. Greenwood was already an established attendee of Winterbottom's coaching courses and in 1953 was a professional player with Chelsea. He appeared to have been absolutely enthralled by the whole experience, describing it as one of the most exciting days of his life. The future was laid out for him with a 'tomorrow's world' opening up.

Interestingly, he didn't see the match or the result in negative terms for England. He interpreted it in more global terms as a great opportunity to learn and develop. It provided him with the experience he'd been waiting for to stimulate his own thoughts on how football should be played. Greenwood saw change, as did Winterbottom, as a long process. For him it was the Hungary performance that acted as confirmation that the game in England had lost decades in development, and it was from this point forward that change could be initiated, in what Greenwood described as revolutionary terms. It was certainly a revolutionary experience for him, but of course, that does not mean it was a revolutionary experience for all. For example, Greenwood interpreted the match differently from many others. He saw the core of Hungary's unbelievable level of play as a combination of passing angles and that the man on the ball had three passing options open to him.

Bobby Robson took over from Greenwood as England manager in 1982. Robson rhapsodised for decades on the brilliance of the Hungarians and the influence they had on him personally. He was a young professional with Fulham in 1953, yet to establish himself in the England team. Robson went to the 6-3 game with a small group of Fulham players led by Jimmy Hill, another individual who was to have a tremendous influence over English football in multiple areas over the next 40 years. Robson took similar conclusions to Greenwood in that it was not so much the result that was important or that affected him, but the performance of the Hungarians. The impact it had on him was fundamental in that it acted as the catalyst for his coaching career. Like Greenwood he'd seen what he interpreted as the future, and he wanted to be a part of that future.

It was soon after the 6-3 game that Robson started attending the FA coaching courses run by Winterbottom at Paddington Street in central London. Among other attendees of those early courses, he cited Hill, Greenwood and Fulham team-mate Jackie Goodwin. Robson felt that the main issues which restricted Winterbottom at this time were the selection of the team by committee with only limited input from the manager and a lack of preparation time for the team despite there being in the early 1950s only two club competitions – the league and the FA Cup.

One of the main draws for Robson in the coaching world was Winterbottom himself. He clearly had nothing but deep respect for Winterbottom as an educator and mentor, in a similar vein to Billy Wright. Robson learned from Winterbottom due to an open mind and respected him as a meticulous professional, an intelligent man with a flair for oration and a considerable depth of knowledge about the game that he could impart fully. Robson saw Winterbottom in very different terms from many other players as he felt he was a down-to-earth type of man who communicated with the regular player in clear and concise language, not the atomic scientist or academic boffin as many characterised him.

Noel Cantwell was another player who attended the 6-3 match and took away a positive outlook. Cantwell was a West Ham player in 1953 and Republic of Ireland international who described the Hungary match as 'almost like a religious experience', given the deep impact it had on him. He was not alone among West Ham players at the game who were deeply affected by it as Malcolm Allison was certainly there and John Bond was another direct disciple of the Hungarian way of playing. The West Ham contingent took their ideas from the 6-3 game and utilised them by endlessly moving around the condiments on the Cassetari Café tables, representing player positions.

Yet more individuals who had a deep impact and influence on the English game both from the past and into the future were part of the 100,000 crowd inside Wembley. Dave Sexton, future manager of Chelsea and the exciting mid-1970s team at Queens Park Rangers, watched the match live as did Jimmy Hogan, who was then Aston Villa's youth team coach after his long, peripatetic coaching career across Europe. Sexton was another of Winterbottom's acolytes on the earlier FA coaching courses and would go on to have a long-standing presence in the FA setup, including as coach of the England under-21 team.

The schoolboys that George Robb taught came in a group with half a day off school to cheer on their PT master.

Even a group of young players from Watford, accompanied by their player-coach Johnny Paton, travelled the relatively short distance to Wembley to observe the Hungarians. Of course, all the major scribes and journalists of the day were ensconced in the press box or dotted around the stadium – Charles Buchan, Geoffrey Green and Willy Meisl, reporting with words that would be repeated endlessly over the next seven decades. On this occasion they were accompanied by the injured Tom Finney though according to the 'Preston Plumber', due to the FA protocol at the time he was not actually allowed to say anything negative about England as part of his contributions to the radio commentary and analysis.

The press interest across Europe was intense with more than 100 foreign journalists at Wembley – including Jacques Ferran from *L'Équipe*, Rudi Eklow, the sports editor of Scandinavia's biggest morning paper, and Dr Friedbart Becker, who was, according to Meisl, Germany's premier soccer journalist. A party of players went down to Wembley from Aston Villa with Peter McParland remembering a team-mate saying to him there was no need to worry about Hungary as, 'They'll be all possession and no shots.'

Even if they couldn't make it to Wembley that day, people experienced the game through film. Sir Alex Ferguson, in his foreword to Gyorgy Szollosi's book on Puskás, admitted that his schoolboy self wagged lessons that afternoon in order to watch the match on television. Sir Alex was another on whom the game had an impact over how he saw football and visualised what was achievable, as he summed it up as a football revolution. All these many characters and mostly future influencers made the effort to attend the match and absorb it. As in any game they all experienced those crucial 90 minutes differently, but they all drank in the Hungarian whirl. They observed and processed the skill level, the accurate passing and off the ball movement of the *Aranycsapat*. Many of the young professionals, among Winterbottom's early coaching cohort, took their enthusiasm, impressions and conclusions out of Wembley and back to their clubs, not just in the immediacy but to coaching and managerial roles making them among the most important and influential individuals in English football for the next three decades and longer.

England's Competitive Record and Team Selection

THE LONG-HAILED record of England never having been defeated at home by a foreign country had gone forever. However, this record itself is not quite the Olympian achievement that it may first appear. The 6-3 game was England's 58th post-World War Two international. Of the previous 57, 25 were at home and 32 were away. Twenty-five of the 57 games were against Scotland (seven), Wales (eight), Northern Ireland (eight) and the Republic of Ireland (two). A total of 44 per cent were still against the four football countries England had always played since 1872. Clearly only 56 per cent were against genuine foreign opposition, as defined at the time. A small selection of western European nations provided the overall majority of opposition. Of the 32 matches against genuine foreigners a total of 15 were split evenly with three each against Switzerland, France, Portugal, Belgium and Italy, with just seven matches against non-European opposition.

Perhaps more surprising is that of the 25 postwar home games up to Hungary in November 1953, only nine were played at Wembley, with four of those against Scotland. In the 1970s to the 1990s virtually every England home game was at Wembley, but this was not the case between 1946 and

186

1953. During this period England played at seven different league grounds around the country – Highbury, Arsenal (five); Goodison Park, Everton (four); Villa Park, Aston Villa (two); Maine Road, Manchester City (two); Leeds Road, Huddersfield (one); White Hart Lane, Tottenham (one); Roker Park, Sunderland (one). From the mid-1950s onwards the move was towards Wembley with this level of geographical dispersion not seen again until the 2000s, in the interregnum period when the new Wembley was constructed.

In addition to the home record perhaps not being quite as impressive as assumed, the England team sent out at Wembley was clearly disparate in the contemporary success of the clubs that the 11 individuals played for. The obvious yardstick for any team's performance at any level in any country in the world is league position. If you look at the final league table for 1952/53 there is a curious underutilisation of players from the top clubs. From the top five finishers – Arsenal, Preston North End, Wolverhampton Wanderers, West Bromwich Albion and Charlton Athletic – only Wolves' Billy Wright was chosen, although Preston's Tom Finney would have played if not injured. Blackpool provided their quartet of players due to a bias towards their FA Cup victory six months earlier. Mortensen and Matthews were regular England selections, but the 6-3 defeat was Ernie Taylor's only England appearance and Harry Johnston never appeared again after it.

The reality was that the bulk of the England team was made up of players who performed for mid-table clubs or, in the case of two players, played in the Second Division. Tottenham Hotspur finished tenth in 1952/53 but provided Alf Ramsey and George Robb. Portsmouth and Sheffield Wednesday struggled in the First Division the previous season, finishing 15th and 18th respectively, from where Jimmy Dickinson and Jackie Sewell were chosen. Gil Merrick and Bill Eckersley played their football in the Second Division for Birmingham City and Blackburn Rovers respectively, both clubs having moderate finishes in 1952/53. In conclusion, a core group of the England team chosen that day were used to performing in unsuccessful, struggling and second-tier clubs and then were picked with a fairly minimal build-up process to face a team on a long unbeaten run.

PART THREE: AFTER

Aftermath

WHEN LEO Horn blew the final whistle, an era had genuinely ended. Hungary were the first truly 'foreign' team to defeat England at home after 24 previous games against continental and, on one occasion, South American opposition. Many times it had been written how England had never been beaten at home by a foreign team until November 1953, which considering their first international was in 1872 appears, in an immediate sense, wholly impressive.

The reality is somewhat different. The Hungary game was only the 25th home match against full foreign opposition – all of them, except for Argentina in May 1951, against European nations. Indeed, England didn't play against a European team at home until hosting Belgium at Highbury in March 1923, and then only one other international against European opposition at home until playing Spain in December 1931. The Golden Age at which Stanley Matthews looked back on of performances and results from the interwar period is actually very difficult to assess due to a lack of games against top foreign opposition.

In the whole interwar period from Belgium in March 1923 to Norway in November 1938 England played just 11 matches against continental European nations at home. England didn't compete in the first three World Cups, due to not being in FIFA, but if you take European nations who finished in at least semi-final positions in the World Cups of 1930, 1934 and 1938 this would include Italy, Yugoslavia, Germany, Czechoslovakia, Austria, Hungary and Sweden. England played these seven top-performing countries at home on just five occasions and none of them more than once. The dominant European team of the 1930s were double world champions Italy, whom England played just once at home pre-1939 in the infamous 'Battle of Highbury' in November 1934, a game that was reputedly more violent than the first round of the 1985 Marvin Hagler v Tommy Hearns superfight.

Even after international football recommenced following World War Two, England only played 12 home internationals against foreign opposition in eight years. Only in 1951 did they play more than two home internationals against foreign teams. The somewhat overstated record had gone two years later and there was no denying that six goals had been conceded at Wembley, something that had never happened before and hasn't happened since. The myth-making of the immediate aftermath started almost as soon as the players left the pitch. As they walked off, the England players at a trudge, there was no violent pitch invasion, no smashing up of the goalposts, individuals didn't appear to confront players with violence in mind, and bottles didn't rain down on the players' heads. All these more extreme responses were for the 1970s and 1980s. The response of a considerable part of the Wembley crowd was to applaud the victors off the pitch. There was a relatively small group of Hungarian fans clustered together, but the vast majority who applauded the Magnificent Magyars were England fans.

As soon as the players vanished from view into the bowels of Wembley stadium the myth-making began.

There was a considerable amount of warmth and generosity shown to the Hungarians from English players, fans and the press after their Wembley victory. They were feted at the official post-match banquet where they were told by FA chairman Amos Brook Hirst that their display was one that everybody should admire. In the December 1953 edition of the *FA Bulletin* an article by A.J. Forrest virtually crowed, '[The] Hungarian triumph was wrested in a manner which caused joy and satisfaction to every connoisseur of football and will be spoken of with admiration in these islands until most heads now young, are smothered grey.' How right he was.

Primary among these myths was the immediate impact this match and result had on the game in England. To read numerous accounts, both contemporary and secondary, it was as if everyone involved in the English game and particularly those inside Wembley that day ran out of the ground and immediately transformed the national approach in a whirlwind revolution. This is not an accurate assessment of what happened. The picture was far more complicated than that, with change taking place at a much slower pace that was more evolution than revolution, and the two distinct camps – the enthusiastic and the doubters – coming to the fore. For some the performance and the result were an inevitability and for others it was a genuine shock, and for another group, particularly some of the press, it was impossible to gauge an accurate assessment due to a colossal *volte-face*. Six months later, almost to the day, England were annihilated 7-1 in Budapest in, statistically, the worst result for the national team. What was the result in practical terms of the myriad of opinions and approaches in those six months? Overall change came in three distinct phases – short, medium and long term.

Overall, there was not even conclusiveness as to what had happened in November 1953 and what its impact would be. In *Football: A Sociology of the Global Game*, Richard Giulianotti concluded that the 6-3 result acquired a level of mythology in the English game so deep that it shook the football traditions of the country to their foundations and forced a rethink of Britain's world status. In a common theme of later writers, Giulianotti drew a distinct parallel between this shock to football status and the 'collapse' of the British Empire as colonies won or were granted their independence. Richard Weight, in his tome *Patriots – National Identity in Britain 1940–2000*, took it a level higher when arguing that Hungary's victory was an Agincourt in reverse and that the significance of this singular event helped 'to alter the trajectory of Britishness'. It was from this match onwards, according to Weight, that 'football began to replace cricket as the game seen by most social classes to embody the nation's character and the game upon which England's international sporting reputation rested'.

From Agincourt in reverse to Alf Ramsey's view that really the Hungarians were just a bit lucky to win by such a convincing scoreline due to a Second Division goalkeeper flapping at a couple of long-range shots, there was a whole range of opinion in between these two extremes.

The semi-myth grew up that the impact of the result of the 6-3 game and particularly the Hungarians' performance led to all the FA committee members rushing back to Lancaster Gate with every league manager in tow to draw up a superplan to immediately revolutionise all aspects of English football. The reality was very different with a mixed bag of responses, developments and denials prevalent to ensure that though change did take place it was of an evolutionary nature.

The most vociferous voice for responsive action came, unsurprisingly, from national press sports journalists. In a U-turn of spectacular proportions that was to become standard down the decades, the press went from insisting that England would swat Hungary aside to concluding, post-match, that the whole world had been turned upside down and that England had to do everything they could to copy every positive element of the Hungarian setup. This explanation would echo down the ages as different European countries dominated international football. All England had to do to reach the top was follow the Germans, French, Dutch or Spanish.

Pre-match the cohort of press, several of whom had seen Hungary's previous match against Sweden in Budapest, argued that the Hungarians had a robotic style that was typical of the communist bloc and this rigidity of approach would be no match for the spontaneity and individual skills of the English players. On the day of the game prominent journalists such as the *Daily Telegraph*'s Frank Coles had categorically stated, 'The Hungarian superb ball jugglers can be checked by firm tackling.' In other words – any fancy dan continental passing and messing about, nail them and there won't be any problems. Unfortunately for England just booting your opponents into submission didn't work.

Though elements of the press called for immediate change and panic, the English reaction was not one of wrath and vengeance but instead an appreciation of Hungary and their performance. After being applauded off the pitch by most of the Wembley crowd, the English showed further appreciation for the *Aranycsapat* when a large crowd of well-wishers cheered the Hungarians farewell at Victoria train station in London. Things appeared to have been rather low-key from a Hungarian perspective. The dressing room was rather quiet with players individually absorbing their achievement with no expansive celebrations. According to Nándor Hidegkuti, the team then went to the nearby Wembley Exhibition Centre to watch an England versus Hungary table tennis competition.

Many historians and social commentators position the 6-3 defeat somewhere within a continuum of the declinism allocated to the destruction of the British Empire from 1945 to around 1970. In this argument the Hungarian defeat stood at the beginning of this process. In 1953, bar the obvious and colossal exception of the Indian subcontinent, the empire remained mostly intact. Intact as a balloon with a pin about to pierce it perhaps, but intact nonetheless. Defeat, destruction, loss, flags being lowered, were all to follow with metronomic regularity in the next 20 years, but this was not the position in 1953. The debacle of Suez, where Britain's belief of top-tier world power status was destroyed in the Sinai desert, was three years away.

The crux of the aftermath was the ongoing split between the changers and those of a status quo outlook. Fundamentally it was all very well that the likes of Ron Greenwood, Bobby Robson or Malcolm Allison were enthused and excited about everything the Hungarians did that November day, but they were players, with only limited influence at their respective clubs. Their time at the pinnacle of management and coaching would come, but in 1953 the immediate power and influence was held in the committee rooms of the Football Association and Football League and their outlook was far from cutting edge.

Media Coverage

CHARLES BUCHAN, who had successfully bridged the gap between playing and journalism, was a focussed observer of the 6-3 game and though his eyes were fully open to the meaning of the teams' performances he wasn't about to lead personal attacks on the players. In the *News Chronicle* he was unequivocal in his assessment that England had been 'outplayed, outgeneraled, outpaced and outshot' and in the subsequent months developed his case as to what had gone wrong and how this was to be remedied. Frank Coles in *The Telegraph* described Hidegkuti's position and role as the withdrawn striker and this was the analysis that stuck – the deep-lying centre-forward.

By January 1954 in *Charles Buchan's Football Monthly*, a more cohesive argument was put forward. Buchan interpreted the defeat as probably being beneficial in the long run as it may bring the jolt required. He advised a radical change in approach to internationals against countries who regarded internationals as of paramount importance. The basis of this had to come through league clubs who needed to develop a complete change in attitude. Buchan's central requirement was that the clubs would put their players at the disposal of the FA, so that they could undergo intensive preparation for the challenges ahead or, as he worded it, 'the tremendous task'. The perfect opportunity, according to Buchan, to initiate this programme would be in a six-week gap between the domestic league season ending and the commencement of the World Cup in the summer of 1954. These intense blocks of training would provide the space and time to develop a more thorough tactical awareness, improve the lack of movement of England players off the ball and develop a clearer defensive understanding to stop the gaps that were so apparent in the games against FIFA and Hungary.

In addition to these technical and tactical changes, Buchan was clear that a change in personnel was required. He argued that England needed a 'general', someone who had been through the trials and tribulations of managing a league side and could get the best out of the players in the limited time periods. Buchan stressed that the core of England's issue was not the quality of players, but the quality of training and preparation. He felt that the players were not clear on their role, within the team. This was a wholesale criticism of Winterbottom and his approach and experience. Buchan even went as far as to state any one of three men who should occupy this role – Jimmy Seed of Charlton Athletic, Tom Whitaker at Arsenal and Stan Cullis at Wolverhampton Wanderers.

A large section of that edition focussed on the aftermath of the 6-3 defeat with accusations and finger-pointing aplenty in an article by John Thompson. Take your pick from the litany of proscribed England failures – the national team was just an irrelevant appendage to the league and cup, there was no preparation, England had refused to learn from the methods developed by foreigners, a rather tangential comment about how league clubs needed to be more active in the care and happiness of boys who lived in their neighbourhoods and a strong castigation of clubs that did not do this. A major point of weakness which, according to Thompson, had to be rectified, was the lack of quick control with England taking multiple touches to control the ball to the Hungarians' single touch. Thompson's assessment of individual England players' performances was fascinating in that it was at odds with the conclusions of other contemporary observers. Among England's most glaring faults was a lack of understanding of players in their positional sense. Thompson rather generously admired Matthews for keeping three Hungarian players busy and Mortensen for his heart and drive. Harry Johnston was identified as a presence who towered defensively above the other England defenders, and it was stressed that if it had not been for Johnston then the Hungarians would have reached double figures. The performances of Wright and Dickinson were interpreted as poor.

This article, slightly removed from the immediacy of the game, brought a very different voice to the aftermath phase. Most others saw Johnston flapping around in no man's land and the player himself recounted his performance as a nightmare; indeed, he never appeared for England again. Interestingly, Thompson blamed the poor defensive performance, on Billy Wright and Jimmy Dickinson, the only outfield players, along with Jackie Sewell, retained in Budapest six months later. Sewell and Ernie Taylor were also considered poor, whereas the limited performance of George Robb was seen with sympathy due to his isolation on the wing and particularly the ever-dependent reliance of wingers for the service of passes from others. If those passes didn't go anywhere near the flying winger then it was a meaningless position, particularly in the rigidity of the English system. If the great Stanley Matthews didn't show any positional flexibility to collect the ball, then why would anyone else?

The multiplicity of responses and arguments at a febrile level faded quickly and, in most forms, business returned to a position of normality or, more accurately, the status quo. The league and the FA Cup were the be all and end all, with internationals popping up periodically and the World Cup an isolated three-week tournament played once every four years. From virtual blanket coverage in the January 1954 edition of *Charles Buchan's Football Monthly*, within a couple of months the inquests and focus on international football had vanished to be replaced by an analysis exclusively of domestic football.

Though, in the immediate aftermath of the game, Billy Wright acknowledged that himself and the English dressing room, presumably except for Alf Ramsey, accepted they had been defeated on the day by a far superior team, he was quick to dispute that anything the Hungarians were doing was new or revolutionary. Wright dismissed this point of view as 'nonsense', although he opined that the Hungarians were a highly skilled team who played as a well-organised unit. According to Wright in *Football is My Passport*, all the Hungarians had done was 'resurrect many of the basic principles which in the prewar period had made English football the most dominating in the world'. It was not made clear which basic principles Wright was referring to, but it's interesting that one of the few points that Wright and Matthews agreed on was the paramount nature of English football in an international context during the interwar period.

The other main point that Wright made to quell the 'sheer nonsense' of the immediate aftermath was that only recently England fans had seen a league team playing in a similar style to the Hungarians – Tottenham Hotspur, who were champions in 1951. Wright argued that the Hungarian emphasis on player movement off the ball was close to the style developed by Arthur Rowe's 'push and run' Spurs team. This begs the obvious and immediate question that if Hungary were, in Wright's opinion, playing a style similar to a high-profile English club side then why was the national team so poor at dealing with the Hungarians defensively, including two players who played for Tottenham – Robb and Ramsey? Wright offered no explanation for this shortcoming but rather moved the blame for a fall in the standards of the international team to a group not actually involved – young players. The Hungarians worked for perfection, but Wright felt a clear explanation for a drop in England's standards was that too many lightweights had been recruited into the fold of professional football, who saw signing a professional contract as a culmination rather than a starting point.

Wright was most certainly in the camp of perceiving the aftermath of the 6-3 defeat as revolutionary not evolutionary, as he claimed that it created a new interest in football with many league teams completely re-planning their training schedules and squads extensively watching film of the match to analyse how the Hungarians played. Wright also stated that the aim of building a superb side to become the equal of the Magyars became an obsession. The focus in England was on the shortcomings of the game and the broad determination to raise the standards of football in a short timeframe. This conclusion by the England captain would have been news to his colleagues Matthews and Ramsey and, indeed, Winterbottom who knew that the widescale implementation of changes he was already making was a longer-term project. Wright stood as a voice for rapid change as 'everyone in England became conscious of our shortcomings and determined to try and raise our soccer standards in the quickest possible time'. This was written in 1957 but it seems that very few on the international selection committee were listening to voices such as their international captain. Even if there was a recognition for change at all levels, it moved in a haphazard manner.

In the pattern of international football, then as now, there are considerable gaps where there are no matches and, effectively, there is little for the manager to do but watch the players walk out of the Wembley changing rooms and return to their clubs. This period of weeks and months would often become one of unlearning what Winterbottom focussed on, to return to the doctrines of their clubs and league football, without even a full debriefing session and, of course, that's if the players were listening in the first place. For six members of the team it made no difference in terms of the international side as they were never selected again.

A gap of three and a half months followed until England's next match, against Scotland, the 71st time they'd met in a full international. There was no requirement to adapt to new systems or new shapes or cutting-edge tactical implementations. Only Merrick, Wright and Dickinson survived and England defeated the Scots 4-2 at Hampden in front of a mega crowd of 134,500. This victory had a double meaning as the final World Cup qualifier. Generously for the home nations, FIFA counted the 1953/54 season Home International Championship as the World Cup qualifying series. England duly topped the group with the victory in Glasgow after a 4-1 victory over Wales in October 1953 and a 3-1 win over Northern Ireland two weeks before the 6-3 defeat.

After qualification, England had two preparation games before their first match in the World Cup, against Belgium on 17 June 1954. First was a very challenging test in Belgrade where most of the team that defeated Scotland were retained, losing 1-0 to Yugoslavia. In overall terms this was not such a poor result, as subsequently, England had a very poor record in Yugoslavia. They had lost there in 1939, would be hammered 5-0 there in 1958 and would not record their solitary win in Yugoslavia until Bobby Robson's tenure with a convincing 4-1 victory in late 1987. Indeed, Winterbottom commented that the worst England performance under his long period as manager was the 5-0 trouncing just before the 1958 World Cup.

A week after losing in Belgrade, England then went to Budapest for the return game to the 6-3 defeat, in their final preparation match for the World Cup. In the months leading up to the 1954 finals someone, somewhere in the corridors and rooms of the Football Association headquarters had the infinitely bright idea to play Hungary in their new super stadium 25 days before the World Cup commenced. If England's 6-3 defeat at Wembley was a disaster, then the 7-1 annihilation in Budapest was a humiliation of an incomparable level. Even Tom Finney, restored to the team after injury in November 1953, said he just wanted the ground to swallow him up in the last 20 minutes.

The core problem was that England approached the second Hungary game in the same way they approached the first – an inexperienced team, playing the same rigid and wholly predictable system and with a relatively short amount of preparation time. The long-held alternative definition of stupidity is to repeat the same actions and decisions that haven't worked and hope that the outcome will be different. This is exactly what England did in their defeat in the Népstadion. The supposed swirling atmosphere of revolution and change in the English game was restricted to a small coterie of journalists and a group of professional players who would later go on to have tremendous influence. Prior to the 1954 World Cup it did not exist in the corridors of power.

Charles Buchan, who'd made his recommendations after the 6-3 game, proposed an even more comprehensive list in his monthly magazine after England conceded seven in Budapest. Buchan lived football and felt it to the core, and commented on this match live. He didn't appear to be aware that his microphone was on continually and he groaned his way through the game as Hungary built attack after attack, in a manner any fan on the terraces would have. In a classic immediate reaction to a disaster his response in his widely read national magazine was to take a sword to almost everyone and everything. In the type of sentiments echoed later in countless football phone-ins, Buchan didn't hold back. He concluded that England were many years behind Hungary in all the essential areas – speed, distribution and teamwork. All had to change with a complete move away from the plodding and complacent approach which existed in too much of the game in England. The small beacons of light were present at Manchester United, Wolverhampton Wanderers, Tottenham and Portsmouth. Buchan went radical in pushing for a Great Britain team as a strong rebuff to a deteriorating worldwide standing, with the international team being prioritised over club football.

This long and conclusive article covered a broad range of points for the development of the game in England at different levels. Tom Finney was quoted as saying that England needed to follow Hungary's approach and have a fundamentally set squad of over 30 players who were kept together for considerable periods of time. Buchan focussed on the new generation of young players and their development. The key to success came from points praised for the Hungarians – quick-thinking, fast-moving and clever players with accurate and close passing. The most important single requirement was to work together for the interests of the national team. Buchan proposed that the most effective solution would be to fundamentally jettison the older players and old approach and focus on youth development. The basis needed to be on the art of positioning, covering and a dramatic speeding up of movements. Buchan made two further interesting arguments for the English game's development – that there had been too much instinctive football and not enough thinking and that the match crowd had an important role to play if England were to improve. He felt the crowd were a negative influence on young players with their shouts of 'get stuck in' and 'get rid of it', and that supporters needed to educate themselves on the finer points of the game and be more patient. Buchan's multilevel assessment was more comprehensive after the Budapest defeat than Wembley. For him the 7-1 destruction confirmed the gulf in London six months earlier and there was now no avoiding the fact that considerable change had to enter the English structure if there was to be any realistic challenge for European or world supremacy. The supertanker needed to change course but the issue, as always, was people such as Buchan were not at the helm.

Billy Wright, as was often the case, was keen to defend Walter Winterbottom from being the target of negative comments. He insisted that preparation for the 7-1 defeat was thorough with special training at Eastbourne where every aspect of the Hungarian performance at Wembley was studied *ad nauseam*. Wright stated that he watched the film of the 6-3 game on so many occasions that he felt he knew the Hungarian players better than any English players he'd lined up against. Not only were England fully prepared for the return match in Budapest, but Wright continued the pattern of the 6-3 reverse by pushing the responsibility of defeat on to others. In a truly mind-blowing piece of paradoxical writing in *Football is My Passport*, Wright said, 'It was not our defensive work or approach work that let us down. Not for the first time finishing – once our greatest strength – had proved to be our weakness.' Part of you just has to admire the spectacular chutzpah of the statement. The main reason that England lost in Budapest in May 1954 wasn't because the defensive unit conceded seven goals, it was because the attacking players didn't score at least eight to ensure victory. Wright was convinced that the two major messages from Budapest were that England could not continue with their scratch team approach and that it was an absolute necessity for sides to return to their strength of first-time shooting.

When Wright spotted Hungarian coach Gusztáv Sebes spying on England's training and preparation, he didn't mention whether his shoulders were shaking with laughter. Sebes was watching intently from a quiet spot, no doubt writing copious notes in his ever-present books. Surely he only needed to stay for five minutes to conclude that England would play in exactly the same way as in London six months previously. The change was in personnel, not tactics or system – Ramsey, Eckersley, Johnston, Matthews, Taylor, Mortensen and Robb were all gone, most of them forever, to be replaced by Staniforth, Byrne, Owen, Harris, Jezzard, Broadis and Finney. In contrast, Hungary changed just one player from the Wembley match with Tóth coming in for Budai. The *Official FA Yearbook of 1954/55* concluded that Hungary were even better in Budapest than London and played football of a supreme order, their greatest attribute being the movement of their entire forward line which led to their seven-goal haul, going so far as to state there were five geniuses in the Hungarian line up.

Whatever level of football you've played at, we've all been destroyed in a game at least once or watched your team destroyed – seven or eight down with ten minutes to go, you enter a new world, a new experience. A world of embarrassment and humiliation where those ten minutes become hours. To experience that at the highest international level in front of 92,000 people, as was the case in Budapest, doesn't bear thinking about. Perhaps for this reason the voice of English players from the Budapest game was restricted in comparison to London. Merrick, Wright and Finney appeared to be the only three who extensively expressed their opinions and recollections of this specific game. In his autobiography from almost 50 years after the match, Finney communicated the utter discombobulation of that performance. Of course, Finney had missed the Wembley game due to injury and had viewed it from the removed position of the press box rather than the maelstrom on the pitch. There was no avoiding his place in the return game, terming it a game of racehorses against carthorses. Finney squarely laid the blame on the bizarre decisions of the international selection committee in choosing players who were just not of the level required. A strange sort of 'team on parade' was how Finney describes the quixotic decisions of the FA.

Finney, at five decades' distance, named those players whose selection clearly caused him concerns – the fantastically named Bedford Jezzard made his debut then didn't make the squad for the World Cup a month later and only ever played once again for England, versus Northern Ireland. Jackie Sewell was not rated as top level by Finney, and neither were full-back Ron Staniforth from Huddersfield, who retained his position for the imminent World Cup, or the Portsmouth winger Peter Harris, who bizarrely returned to international football after a four-and-a-half-year gap. His only other international was the September 1949 defeat to Eire. He never played for England again after Budapest, completing a thoroughly horrendous couple of games to be involved in. Finney was categorical, though polite, that he didn't rate them at all, 'They were not household names [somewhat unfair on Jackie Sewell] or international players of stature and Budapest was not the right occasion for experimenting.'

The selection committee certainly got it all wrong. In terms of internationals going into the Budapest game, Finney was correct – Jezzard was making his debut, Staniforth was playing his third game for England, Sid Owen his second, Roger Byrne his third, Harris his second and Sewell his sixth. In conclusion, six of the team walking out on to the pitch at the Népstadion had 11 previous England appearances between them. The selectors thought it through and decided to send a side out against the world's best team playing at home with half of them owning less than a dozen appearances.

The performance of such a mish-mash of a team was surely totally predictable. Finney was more open in his long-delayed conclusions and points than the other players, Merrick and Wright, who recorded their views in a period reasonably close to the game. He was certainly more realistic than Wright in saying the issues in Budapest were not defensive. England played like a group of strangers, which was exactly what they were, and Finney emphasised that they were a set of individuals who went about their business with no connection to those around them. In contrast Hungary played their team-based game with its quick passing moves and movement off the ball.

The outlandish selection – can you even apply the word policy – continued apace after the Budapest match. As in London six months earlier several players found that they had either played their last game or they would be gone in the next few matches, particularly after the looming Swiss World Cup. Gil Merrick was made a scapegoat after Budapest and Switzerland and never played again after the World Cup quarter-final, the 4-2 defeat to Uruguay. Sewell never played for England again, his last two appearances being the double Hungarian catastrophes. Ron Staniforth played all three games in that summer's World Cup, but only lasted until October 1954 when he featured in a home win over the newly crowned surprise world champions West Germany and never played after that. Syd Owen played just once more after the Budapest annihilation, the 4-4 draw against Belgium in the World Cup four weeks later. Peter Harris's rather bizarre two-game England career also came to an end in Budapest.

Perhaps no player's situation epitomises the ridiculous nature of the selection committee more than that of Harris. Two caps for England, almost six years and 39 internationals apart, then being dropped again, this time for eternity, not even making the squad for the World Cup that followed four weeks after his second cap. Considering the Budapest match was the last one before the World Cup that summer, of the England XI that day, three weren't just dropped from the team, they didn't even make the squad – Harris, Sewell and Jezzard. In an echo of the 6-3 Wembley defeat only four players were retained in the longer term to really continue their England careers – Billy Wright, Jimmy Dickinson, Tom Finney and Roger Byrne.

The press response to the 7-1 defeat followed the pattern of the 6-3 six months earlier. There was none of the pure vitriol and hatred that would come in later decades, but there was an air of embarrassment and a certain sadness, and the overriding factor reported was of awe for the Hungarians and their performance and either no or a restricted negative criticism for Winterbottom. The *Daily Mail* went as far as to state that the Magical Magyars were from another planet. Winterbottom was reported on the flight home as being calm and accepting of the result and Hungary's performance.

In a sense, of course, Winterbottom knew exactly what was coming in Budapest. England had conceded six at home so was it such a surprise they would ship seven, that could have been ten, in the Népstadion, playing in the same outmoded style, in the same outmoded kit, with a second series of inexplicable and illogical selection decisions from the committee? Was there ever going to be any other result than the one that happened? In an interesting paradox, though Winterbottom clearly wanted more input and control over selection, it always gave him an out. He made it clear after most of the major defeats that there were certain players, such as George Robb in the 6-3 defeat, who were not his choice. It is difficult to believe that Winterbottom would have chosen to bring in Peter Harris from five years in the international wilderness to face Hungary. Everyone knew that Winterbottom didn't have sole control over team selection, so he couldn't have been held solely responsible for decisions that weren't his. The responsibility faded away into the ether of the faceless committee members who most fans didn't know from Adam. How do you rain down vitriol when you don't know who you're aiming it at?

Gil Merrick was one of the few players involved who commented at the time, in his 1954 half autobiography, half goalkeeping manual *I See it All*. He openly stated that when Hungary scored three goals in six minutes to make it 6-0 with a quarter of the game remaining he was somewhat terrified to contemplate what the final score might be. Merrick never appeared to be a slouch on self-promotion, as he rather paradoxically claimed that it was only down to him that the score was not double figures. A rather brazen statement for a goalkeeper who'd conceded seven in a match. The only area where, Merrick felt, England surpassed Hungary was in stamina, which beautifully summed up the gap between the teams. Merrick estimated that Hungary did not do a quarter of the running that England did as they controlled the game and moved the ball around, while England's players were endlessly chasing around the pitch. It's very difficult to interpret what Merrick's point is here. Was he being critical of England or was he praising their tenacity?

For Merrick, it was Wembley all over again with Hungarian movement and patterns in front of him weaving confusion among the English defence, only even more comprehensively than six months previously. Realistically how could any goalkeeper survive after conceding 13 goals in two matches? Merrick hung on until the World Cup in the summer but his performances against Belgium and Uruguay, where he conceded another eight goals in total, led to some highly critical comments from Winterbottom, who more than hinted that it was down to Merrick's performances that England failed in Switzerland. Clearly this was not the full case, and it seems Winterbottom wanted to lay it on thick to ensure that the 4-2 defeat to defending champions Uruguay was Merrick's last England appearance. The other members of the selection committee were either listening to Winterbottom's diatribe or had reached the same conclusion themselves.

Merrick couldn't really have any complaints about being replaced by Ray Wood of Manchester United and Bert

Williams of Wolverhampton Wanderers. He had played in all ten of England's internationals in the 1953/54 season and had conceded an incredible 30 goals across the campaign. In addition to the 13 against Hungary, there was also four in a game on three separate occasions against the Rest of Europe, Belgium and Uruguay. Though Merrick was clear that though the defensive personnel was different from Wembley, the defensive tactical approach was the same. In his opinion there were no lessons learned in practical terms. Winterbottom's lack of control over several major aspects of his job, team selection and thorough preparation time were only to be exacerbated in Budapest. He knew, as Merrick hinted, that what awaited England at the Népstadion was certain catastrophe. There was only ever going to be one outcome and, perhaps, Merrick was correct that England were fortunate that they didn't concede double figures.

Willy Meisl, ever ready with a comment and analysis, put it succinctly by concluding that England's tactical approach was exactly the same in Budapest as in London. Meisl cut to the chase and stated that England's problems were multifaceted – insularity, resistance to reforms and a refusal to break with outdated methods encompassing training to tactics. Meisl reinforced his argument with a sprinkling of the excruciating headlines from the English national newspapers on the day of the match, which begs the question, did any of those journalists and sports editors see the 6-3 defeat? With comments such as 'Speed will conquer Puskás and co', 'Jet Jezzard our secret weapon' and 'Our top boys will whip Hungary' it appeared that Fleet Street had certainly not learned any lessons from Hungary's previous victory. Indeed, such an overconfident and misplaced arrogance followed by the immediate and sweeping negativity after an incomparable defeat, set a template for the interpretative path of English newspapers and media in general for decades to come. Meisl's extensive knowledge of continental football put paid to such ridiculous headlines by focussing on Hungary's cerebral play and, as he defined it, perfect technique placed against England's 'unimaginative soccer robots'.

Billy Wright was the epitome of the England team in the 1950s. This was not just because he was the captain and played in almost every international during the 1950s, but of what he represented – the do-or-die attitude and the honest yeoman. In the *Daily Express*'s *The Wright Cuttings Book*, the effect on Wright of the Budapest destruction was clear, 'Billy Wright came off with his face as white as his shirt and looking like a man who has seen a ghost come back to haunt him. As hard as this giant-hearted man tried, he could not get near to suppressing the irrepressible Puskás.' The gulf between Hungary and England was succinctly described. England were lion-hearted and tried their best in their limited approach but were no match for the individual skills and team play of Hungary.

In a similar way to England's defeat to the USA in Brazil four years earlier, the Budapest result went a little bit under the radar due to the fact it was abroad, but also because it was superseded in the contemporary sporting mythology by Roger Bannister, who just two weeks earlier had broken through the sub-four-minute-mile barrier. The contrast was the interest in the match in Hungary which was paramount. There were apparently a million people applying for tickets in the Népstadion. Goalkeeper Gyula Grosics was of the view that the Budapest match was more important than Wembley, as it confirmed that the performance of the *Aranycsapat* was not a one-off result.

Meisl's Response

AMONG THE major voices who had long been outlining the inadequacies of British football was Dr Willy Meisl, mostly through *World Sports Magazine* of which he was the editor. In the January 1954 edition Meisl exposed, in detail, England's shortcomings and brought forward a seven-point plan that would need to be implemented if they were to compete effectively at the highest international level.

Meisl was the self-proclaimed 'world's number one soccer critic' who was no stranger to hyperbole. He argued that the 6-3 defeat was England's 'punishment for the betrayal of the game'. The specific problem was the lack of progression in Britain since the change in the offside rule in 1925 and the insularity which followed. That had brought a blinkered approach in not assessing and analysing the play and systems, at different times, of Austria, Yugoslavia and Czechoslovakia.

Meisl even stated that British correspondents should have gone to see and learn from the Brazilians. Meisl did acknowledge that there was a small cohort who had a wider perspective and would be crucial in changing things. He certainly saw Stanley Rous as the pivotal figure in the administration of football in England, who could be ably assisted in updating English football by this small group, including Arthur Rowe, Matt Busby, Walter Winterbottom and Jimmy Hogan. Although this plan would have appeared radical in 1954, several of the points would be implemented over time.

Meisl's plan was:

1. Deficiencies are at club level. Too much reliance on a game centred on hard tackling and getting stuck in, need to move away from this approach.
2. Force club directors to put country before club.
3. First Division to be cut from 22 to 16 teams.
4. Promotion and relegation to move to four up and four down.
5. Managers to have more specific contracts to give them power and to scrap the international selection committee. Walter Winterbottom to be a true soccer chief for two years.
6. Start to improve basic techniques – ball control.
7. Should be reform at the top as well as at grassroots.

In reality it was a plan mixed with specifics and vague ideas, and some points never came to fruition. The glacial pace of change at the FA and Football League certainly meant that even decades later the specific situation hadn't changed completely. For example, point two – prioritising country over club – was an argument that went on *ad nauseam* through the national management of Don Revie, Ron Greenwood, Bobby Robson and Graham Taylor.

Meisl concluded that the blame should have mostly been with club directors who prioritised their own results in the endless hurly-burly of the league programme and had no concern or interest for the international team, and that this total focus on short-termism led to a lack of tactical development or initiation of new systems.

It is true to say that Meisl had been banging on for a considerable amount of time about the inadequacies of the English game and as far as he was concerned the 6-3 defeat proved everything he had been saying. The insularity, the lack of interest in anything outside Britain, the poor passing, the acceptance by the paying crowd of poor standards, the previous miserable performances by the English national side including recently against Northern Ireland on 11 November 1953 and that 99 per cent of English press and 90 per cent of English football fans had forecast a win for England over Hungary – all these points were reiterated by Meisl to reinforce his argument that this defeat and the style of defeat were inevitable and it was the absolute wake-up call that England needed.

FA Meeting in December 1953

THE MINUTES and proceedings of the Council of the Football Association from 14 December 1953 offer a dry and global football riposte to some of the more lurid conclusions of the revolutionary impact of the 6-3 game. In this meeting, held in the rooms of Lancaster Gate, there was certainly no revolutionary response. It's difficult to sense that any form of evolution was present at all. No one was throwing desks about stressing the need to immediately overhaul the entire footballing structure. You get the impression that bourbon biscuits being put out instead of custard creams would have elicited a stronger reaction. There was no one drawing complex diagrams resembling those from Gusztáv Sebes's notebook on a blackboard. There was a ticking clock in the corner and the clinking of coffee cups, as this powerful and influential council covered a myriad of football-related issues, but not the Hungarians' performance at Wembley or the humiliation seen by all.

For example, the first item on the agenda was a list of gifts received by the FA from other associations commemorating its 90th anniversary. This had been the reason for the Wembley match against the FIFA select team in October 1953. Diligently recorded was a comprehensive list starting with a 1712 map of Germany from the DFB and a selection of silver bowls, plaques and salvers from the likes of Northern Ireland, Austria, Norway, Scotland and the United Gold Coast.

The mechanics of the FA's responsibilities in the 6-3 match were recorded at council level. The selection committee, of which Walter Winterbottom was a removed part as he often attended but was not actually a member – that was left to the likes of chair H. Shentall, C. Hirst, D.F. Wiseman, J.H.W. Mears and H. French – were the hidden men, the ghosts of Lancaster Gate, who decided whether Harry Johnston should be brought back to international football or not, and should Matthews be retained or dropped yet again? Was Gil Merrick the number one goalkeeper in England or was it Wolverhampton Wanderers' Bert Williams?

In time all these questions and burdens would be placed exclusively on the likes of Winterbottom, Alf Ramsey and Don Revie. In 1953 they were still the domain of a group of men with affiliations to specific league clubs with their own clear agendas and limited experiences. How many games did they see of the players they were picking? If they didn't go to Blackpool to see the Wizard play or catch up on the performances of Taylor, Johnston and Mortensen, how did they know whether they were on top form or not? The answer, of course, is that they didn't. Names were plucked from the well of mediocrity because they'd had three good games on the run.

Attention in the council meeting did turn to the 6-3 match. There was no assessment or inquest of the game itself or how Hungary had managed to waltz through the English team so easily. The council was instead concerned with the logistics. However, there were important facts recorded – that the team originally selected six days beforehand was with J. Trotter of Charlton Athletic as trainer and three reserves named to travel with the party, these being Bert Williams, J. Kennedy of West Bromwich Albion and H. Hassall from Bolton Wanderers. Tom Finney was originally listed as the outside-left, confirming the haste with which George Robb was drafted into the team after Finney's injury. On a more prosaic level the central bands of the RAF and the Women's RAF were engaged for a fee of £160 and the match ball boys were provided by the Essex County FA.

The myriad of responsibilities of the FA council were apparent through the range of topics covered in this, no doubt, rather mind-numbing meeting. All possible areas of the game were covered – schools, amateur, the FA Cup, coaching, lectures, disciplinary committee, match and grounds committee, publications committee, youth, benevolent fund and finances. The international team's performance was just one part of the FA's web of involvement which was given no priority over any other element. There was no specific match report presented, no conclusions, no plan, no recommendations, no development and no revolution.

FA Yearbook

IN A sister document produced by the Football Association there was a broader look into the 6-3 game, and some core conclusions drawn. The *Official FA Yearbook*, published by Naldrett Press, covered all aspects of domestic football. Stanley Rous would use this media form as a personal soap box for important issues in the game with an open letter approach entitled 'John Bull'. In the 1954 published edition he turned his attention to the double defeats to the Hungarians and the pre-World Cup loss to Yugoslavia. In a thorough three-page article Rous framed these defeats as a shock, which to him they were not at all. Perhaps the scale of the 7-1 devastation in Budapest was a shock to the system but not the defeat itself.

Rous reiterated the lessons that needed to be learned from Wembley, Budapest and Belgrade, and took a long-term view with a thorough examination of shortcomings and a comprehensive plan laid out, in order for England to retrieve their mastery in the future. Rous repeatedly stressed the longer term and that there was no magic-wand solution that would bring international football to a level that he perceived England played at in the past. Though, just like Stanley Matthews, he didn't explain what he meant by the period of past masters. Rous was clear that as it would take time to regain their position at the summit England's fall didn't happen overnight either, but was the consequence of years of internal stasis and an international expansion in football to a point where it had become a true world game.

Rous was a progressive with a great deal of power in football. So, when he was writing an article in a published book with a national reach, he wasn't a hackneyed Fleet Street journalist with a knee-jerk reaction, he was a key individual who could promote positive change. Rous opened his argument by stressing that fans in England must be realistic about the national team's place in the football pyramid due to new developments in other countries. The innovations that had particularly impressed him were that foreign clubs were inclusive with large memberships, an investment level surpassing anything in the United Kingdom with impressive new stadia being built in countries such as Argentina and Chile, and the rather overarching point that football was taken seriously in other countries.

In conjunction with this increase in standards abroad was the fall in standards in England for which Rous brought forward a range of explanations and responses. Rous argued for changes in approaches at different levels of the game, both macro and micro. He pushed for a coaching focus on more skilful ball control and enhanced preparation for the national team with longer pre-match get-togethers. Rous then made a rather obvious criticism of his colleagues at the FA by stating that football administration in England was designed for a different age. Of course, there is little denying that what Rous wrote was true, but it can't have gone down well with the representatives of the FA committee members, the mythical blazer brigade. This point was further expanded by Rous as he claimed that the whole football system had grown in a haphazard manner, which was a damning indictment of the leadership over decades of the FA and the Football League.

Rous then moved his attention to more global societal issues that he felt had an important impact on the English game and level of performance. He was keen to point out that there were fewer spaces in 1954 for boys to play on, a difficult point to prove, and that the increase in road traffic, through the rise in private car ownership, made football on the streets more restricted. An interesting point, but surely one that could equally apply to any of the western European economies, Italy and West Germany for example, that were experiencing the golden age of wage increase, job stability and consumerism. The explosion in private vehicle ownership didn't happen in the 1950s in European communist countries, but on this point Rous was talking more in terms of sport at the community level than elite competitors. Billy Wright had connected the points of materialism affecting elite participation but, of course, there is a ten-to-15-year delay in this process, even if there is a connection. If a ten-year-old boy in 1954 wasn't interested in playing football due to other material distractions or restrictions on playing spaces, in terms of the elite international team this would not have an effect until around 1968 to 1974.

Rous was concerned with the absolute global nature of the game, so he was interested in football at the community level just as much as the performances in the World Cup. The future of football, according to Rous, was fully dependent on how seriously the community was prepared to encourage sport and the ability to develop new ideas. Football clubs had a clear role and responsibility in this area, Rous stressed, as he pointed out that they did not serve the specific or full needs of their communities. Rous was keen to project a modernist, almost inclusive, approach deeply at odds with the wholly exclusive history of the FA and its ruling council up to that point.

1954 World Cup

WHERE COULD England go after the Budapest defeat, another loss to a communist country in their preparation games for the first European-based World Cup they had competed in? One of those defeats was of a devastating nature. The lessons of the rigidity and inadequacy of England's play had not been taken on board by the selection committee. There was, clearly, not going to be any radical change in approach or shape in the 25 days between the destruction of Budapest and the first game of the World Cup in Switzerland, against Belgium. The committee responded in the way they knew best after a defeat, and just changed the personnel. The hammer came down and out went Peter Harris, Jackie Sewell and Bedford Jezzard to be replaced by Stanley Matthews, Nat Lofthouse and Tommy Taylor. Fundamentally a change of attacking personnel, not defensive; indeed the defence remained the same and promptly conceded another four goals. An international defence that had conceded seven in its previous game was kept together in the same system. Fortunately for the defence the attacking element of the team came through with four goals for a rather bizarre result of a 4-4 draw.

The 1954 World Cup has a low-key presence in contemporary accounts of the England players involved and the journalists of the mid-1950s. Perhaps even the term 'World Cup' for the 1954 tournament is somewhat of a misnomer. Of the 16 countries who qualified, 11 were from Europe. Perhaps the rather long-winded 'European Nations Tournament plus Brazil and Uruguay' would have been a more accurate term, with Mexico, Turkey and South Korea there strictly to make up the numbers.

Even the qualification phase was heavily weighted to Europe with just three entrants from North and Central America, four from South America and three from Asia. Bizarrely Hungary, most analysts' pre-tournament favourites and the reigning Olympic champions, qualified without playing a single game. They were drawn in a two-team qualification group with Poland, who subsequently withdrew, so got an automatic bye to the finals.

Pre-tournament expectation from journalists brought the whole range of opinions to the table. An agenda of patriotism and writing for a home readership must surely have dictated the editor Peter Pringle's opinion in *The Boys' Book of Soccer for 1954* as he proclaimed, 'If either England or Scotland strike their best form in the 1954 World Cup we should see Britain once again the leading football nation in the world.'

Charles Buchan was somewhere in the middle when he ranked the potential contenders to win the tournament and rather diplomatically placed England in sixth, a position where he could include them as possible winners to satisfy his home readership, but in a list behind Hungary, Uruguay, West Germany, Brazil and Austria. Realistically, Buchan was saying England stood virtually no chance.

In contrast to the position of Pringle was the negative but certainly more accurate assessment of the self-proclaimed world football authority, Willy Meisl. In a list of skills required for top teams that Meisl drew up it was clear that England were missing most of them – excellent individual ball control, intelligent positional play when not in possession, precision passing and a cohesion and mutual understanding within the team. Meisl also presciently predicted that Hungary may well not win the tournament as he stated in June 1954, that it might just be too much for them and the continuation of their long unbeaten run.

Despite England's relatively poor showing at the 1954 World Cup it was at this tournament that a slight change of outlook began. In 1950, none of the England party had stayed behind to watch and learn from the other teams in the tournament, but in 1954 it was different. The ease of travelling to Switzerland rather than Brazil was a factor. However, it was not just the journalists reporting on the latter stages of the tournament who stayed, but the selectors, Winterbottom and some of the players, Wright and Finney among them.

Matt Busby, one of the pioneers of a more open approach to the European and world game, had attended the tournament to assess developments. Busby certainly went to the World Cup to study specific training methods and match preparation. He was an admirer of the Hungarians and saw it as a travesty when this superb team surprisingly lost to West Germany in the final. Wright was quite open about England's level of performance in the tournament and concluded that their shortcomings were due largely to playing as individuals rather than as a unit. In his opinion this was because the domestic game was based on individuals creating chances.

The key to the final was always assessed as the fitness of Ferenc Puskás. He had been injured, deliberately he claimed, by the West Germans in Hungary's resounding 8-3 group victory. Was it all deliberate? The vagaries of qualification for the second phase of this World Cup meant that West Germany would always progress through victory over the no-hopers of Turkey, so the result against Hungary was basically an irrelevance. This meant that West Germany missed both Brazil, Willy Meisl's favourites for the tournament, and Uruguay, the defending champions. Gusztáv Sebes, who was forced to resign immediately after the tournament, felt the real reason Hungary failed at the last hurdle was down to nerves. The level of expectation, the long unbeaten run, the pressure of always having to not just win but to be brilliant in victory – everything combined to present what Sebes described as an ultimate test of nerves. Perhaps it was an element of arrogance; after all, Hungary had destroyed West Germany only 14 days before. Their first defeat in four years brought about probably the only genuine surprise winners of a World Cup.

The major international football competition has often been a melting pot for ideas, the confirmation of where you are on the world stage and the rise and fall of individuals, ultimately being a logical point to end many international careers. The 1953/54 season had been like no other for England. Their overall record showed a previously unprecedented four defeats, conceding four goals or more in five out of ten matches. Of their four victories, three came in the annual Home International Championship which doubled as the qualification group for the World Cup, and the only other win was against a fairly weak Swiss team who qualified as World Cup hosts and who later conceded seven to Austria in their quarter-final. By the season's close almost all the starting XI from the 6-3 defeat by Hungary had seen their international careers ended. Even then, only Wright, Dickinson and Matthews played again for England after that summer's quarter-final defeat to Uruguay.

The combination of results over 1953/54 had shown that, surely, change had to come with an appreciation that clearly there were several countries – Hungary, Brazil and Uruguay for certain – who were better trained, better prepared and had more individual skill than England. The picture was as confusing as ever with a web of opinions and outlooks, but at least a discussion was now genuinely taking place. The tragedy of the 1950 World Cup was not that England lost to the United States, but that this specific result was deemed such an off-the-scale fluke that basically nothing happened consequently. The group of performances and results of 1953/54 showed that 'flukes' could no longer be held as a fundamental explanation to what had happened in world football. The response, as ever, was mixed – there was no revolution, but the slow-moving evolution gained more converts and supporters than just the cohort of Winterbottom followers and a few isolated voices in the press.

The complex position abounded between conservatives and progressives later in 1954 when there was a further England v Hungary clash, this time at club level when in October Wolverhampton Wanderers hosted Honvéd at Molineux. This was an important game for England and Wolves captain Billy Wright who was keen to establish that an English team could be competitive against European opposition. Hungary and Honvéd's roles overlapped considerably as a core of players performed for both teams. Close to 55,000 spectators filled Molineux to watch the champions of England attempt to restore some pride. On a specifically designed quagmire of a pitch, watered to produce a surface of lakes and mud, Wolves came out 3-2 victors. The importance of the contest was stressed by its appearance on television as a floodlit game, a rare occurrence in 1954. Stan Cullis, the Wolves manager and ex-England captain, brought a deeply nationalistic element to the contest and was absolutely focussed on showing the Hungarians were not supermen at all, but a team that could be contained, neutralised and beaten, although Honvéd had become almost a roadshow team, like Santos later did, playing matches across Europe on a regular basis.

Geoffrey Green, for one, appeared to have been an admirer of Cullis's approach. He stressed in *Soccer: The World Game* that the key to Wolves' victory was the quick, long movements – the long ball – which reduced the effectiveness of the Hungarian passing game. Not only was play quick back to front, but also from side to side with interchange of passes from wing to wing. Green congratulated Cullis for having a specific plan which was based on these characteristics and developed from the material that was available to him. Of course, the time-honoured truism is always that it's a lot easier to develop a plan with the hours of managing a club team than an international one.

The 'kick and rush' moniker that has been consistently affixed to Cullis's Wolves team is a somewhat simplistic one and doesn't give an accurate picture of play. Wolves were a highly disciplined team where the focus was on getting the ball forward as quickly as possible and focusing play in the opponents' half of the pitch. In complement to this attacking strategy was the expressed defensive plan of a smothering defence and a pressing approach, forcing an opponent to make mistakes. Cullis brought this system to fruition with support from Charles Reep, who statistically analysed hundreds of games and concluded that the long ball or long pass – he termed them 'reachers' – was the most effective attacking strategy for any team. Reep's statistical and fieldwork data may well have been fundamentally flawed, as Jonathan Wilson argued in *Inverting the Pyramid*, but the point was that plans, ideas, data and coaching were being introduced into the English game slowly and surely, to alter the status quo in terms of training and outlook.

Wolves v Honvéd was a game of two distinct halves. Interestingly only the second half was covered on television, and this was when Wolves dominated, adding to the significance of the performance and the result to English fans around the country. The first half was clearly dominated by the short passing game of Honvéd and then the heavy watering made the pitch cut up and the long passing game of Wolves came to the fore as they turned a two-goal deficit into a 3-2 victory.

The most eloquent of writers on English football in the 1950s, Geoffrey Green, saw Wolves as one of a cluster of clubs, including Tottenham Hotspur, who brought forward a different approach to the game away from the *idée fixe* of WM rigidity from the interwar period. Green argued in *Soccer: The World Game* that what was important and successful about Wolves' approach was that the long movements, as he called them, due to speed of play, caught the opposing defence in a state of fluidity. According to Green the wingers, Mullen and Hancocks, were key pieces in the plan. However, these wingers were different from Matthews as they added to the speed and flow of attacking play rather than slowed play down, as was Billy Wright's perennial complaint of the Wizard. Green succinctly summed it up when he wrote, 'Style is based on a plan and a plan is based on the characteristics and ability of the material available.'

The adaptability and focus of a small number of teams, certainly including Wolves, was a form of beacon for Green. He said that English football had to look to develop and adapt with further experimentation and a new tactical outlook for attack. The static situation for the British game up to this point could be exemplified in Green's point that the only widespread developments seen since the change in the offside rule in 1925 were the long throw-in and the third back defensive approach.

Pride is always an important issue and England's pride had been destroyed by the two Hungarian defeats at international level. Wolves' aim to try and earn some pride back was to a certain extent achieved on the night, not just to the packed live crowd but for many watching on television. Indeed, its very presence on television reinforced the importance of the match to the nation, as this was a highly unusual event. Cullis was ecstatic after the victory, stating it was 'the most exciting match I ever saw' and that it was the greatest moment in his club career. Cullis also couldn't resist putting the boot in on Winterbottom, who he didn't see as the right man to be England manager.

The reaction of the popular press in England was predictably jingoistic and somewhat over the top as they proclaimed Wolves the club champions of Europe, if not the world, based on the performance and result of this one match. No one in England mentioned or seemed concerned that the supermen of Honvéd had lost recently to Partizan Belgrade, who were seventh in the Yugoslav league. What mattered to the English football fan was the genuine interconnectedness between Honvéd and the Hungarian national team which had been two-time destroyers of England in the previous 12 months. Six of those destroyers played at Molineux for Honvéd and the resonance of those names etched deep into the minds of home fans being on the receiving end of a defeat from a true English club playing a true English style was what was important.

Hyperbole aside, Wolves v Honvéd was important for two main reasons – its presence as a high in the continuum of increased contact between English and continental clubs and as a partial stimulus to the creation of the European Champion Clubs' Cup. The friendlies between British and European clubs had increased in their regularity since the famous Dynamo Moscow tour in 1945. The appetite for the English supporter to watch and experience foreign opposition had grown in the immediate postwar period. Wolves themselves had played and defeated Spartak Moscow 4-0 only a few weeks before the Honvéd match, but they were not alone. Major London clubs led the way with West Ham, Chelsea, Arsenal and Tottenham Hotspur hosting AC Milan, Hapoel Tel Aviv, Racing Club de Paris and Vörös Lobogó (now MTK Budapest) between them in the early 1950s.

The floodlit friendlies were exciting but random, and momentum was generated for a more structured competition involving Europe's elite club sides on a regular basis. The English press had been overly effusive in their praise of Wolves' victory over Honvéd and had extrapolated the term 'European champions' from one thrilling performance, but Willy Meisl, for one, wasn't having any of it. He acknowledged Wolves' victory but in the homest of home conditions with a grossly and purposely overwatered pitch, which negated the Magyars' intricate passing game. Meisl in *Soccer Revolution* described the pitch as a quagmire and paraphrased Winston Churchill to conclude, 'Rarely in soccer have so many [experts] known so little about recent sports history.' Meisl was all for a broader competition to ascertain a more genuine champion club of Europe. He provided a list of clubs who, he felt, had just as valid a claim to be the top side in Europe or even the world – Real Madrid, AC Milan, Glasgow Rangers, Athletic Bilbao, Corinthians of São Paulo and Flamengo from Rio de Janeiro. In a rather paradoxical development, the very fact that the English popular press unilaterally appointed Wolverhampton Wanderers as European champions became a considerable factor in the momentum for the founding of the European Cup.

The ball was rolling with influential journalists such as Meisl and Gabriel Hanot furthering the case that if there was to be a team claiming European champion status then the time had come for a genuine Europe-wide competition to validate such a title. Hanot was a former French international who wrote in the national country's sports newspaper *L'Équipe* that there should be an officially organised tournament so that whether the team was from Madrid, Milan or Moscow they were genuinely and accurately entitled to call themselves European champions. In an interesting parallel to the founding of the World Cup it was a journalist, not the authorities or a high-ranking football official, who became the focus for change, as Hanot called a meeting to discuss the project in Paris. A total of 15 European clubs attended this monumental gathering. FIFA gave its blessing, but was not the instigator, and in a short timeframe invitations were sent out to several of Europe's elite clubs to participate in the new knockout tournament and by September 1955 the European Champion Clubs' Cup, in the first of its many formats, was up and running.

The first season of competition was based on invitation rather than specific qualification, which produced rather paradoxical situations for the original competitors. There were 18 clubs across Europe who were invited to compete. Unfortunately for Wolves, the defending English champions, it was not they who were invited but the current league leaders Chelsea. Though he abhorred swearing, the language in Stan Cullis's office must have been industrial to say the least. In the short term it didn't really matter too much as, although

Chelsea were crowned league champions for the first time in 1955, they were put under considerable pressure from the Football League not to compete in the first European Cup.

In England, involvement in this new pan-European competition stood at the crossroads between the developers and the statics. Alan Hardaker, the secretary of the Football League, was the static of the statics. From his office in the league's headquarters in Preston he proclaimed that Chelsea shouldn't enter this new, French-initiated competition and they duly complied. Hardaker was concerned about the impact on the Football League's programme and that the advent of extra European club competitions would create fixture congestion, an argument that had momentum for decades to come. Hardaker won for a year but the following season the new champions Manchester United were enthusiastic to take up the European challenge. Matt Busby had always been a keen follower of European football. He had been a direct and interested observer of matches at the 1954 World Cup and he wanted to participate in the genuine challenge of the English champions playing the other top teams in Europe on an annual basis.

The innovators were slowly altering the landscape and pushing the iceberg of the statics in the direction they wanted to go – new challenges and development and integration into the broader football universe. Busby was canny enough to stress to the Manchester United hierarchy that a welcome bonus would be the considerable increase in revenue from the large crowds wanting to see champion teams from Italy, Spain or West Germany. The United secretary Harold Hardman was convinced and the annual European journey began. A new revenue stream was deemed of considerable importance for clubs potentially qualifying for the European Cup and in the years after, the Inter-Cities Fairs Cup and the

European Cup Winners' Cup. Crowds for Football League matches had dropped considerably from what would turn out to be the zenith of the late 1940s. Clearly, however, the option for increased revenue through the European competitions realistically only applied to top-division clubs.

Though the early 1950s had revelled in the performances of the Hungarian national team and Honvéd, it was not the *Mitteleuropa* club sides who dominated the European Cup but instead those from the Mediterranean nations. Indeed, in the first 11 seasons of the European Cup the winners were from just three countries – Spain, Portugal and Italy. The Hungarian age of European dominance had already faded by 1955 and 1956 to the point that a Hungarian club has never won the European Cup or Champions League. The early dominance by Mediterranean clubs lasted until 1967 when Glasgow Celtic defeated Internazionale in Lisbon, which then led to a near 20-year domination by clubs from Britain, the Netherlands and West Germany up to Juventus's 1-0 defeat of Liverpool in the mayhem of Heysel in 1985.

In the pantheon of European Cup winners there was never any place for Honvéd or subsequently any other Hungarian team. The Hungarians had reached their high point just before the European club competitions started, and their shock defeat to West Germany in the 1954 World Cup Final fell as an all-encompassing shadow over the nation's football. They were never able to attain those heights again. After the World Cup defeat, Gusztáv Sebes resigned and as the halo of the players slipped, their special status and privilege did too. Questions were asked about their unique position, and actions that the Communist Party had previously turned a blind eye to, such as smuggling items into the country from foreign tours, now came under scrutiny. Two years later, in 1956, its society was torn apart by the USSR invasion in order to suppress the Hungarian revolt and bring the country back into line with its Warsaw Pact partners. Star player Puskás had had enough and after numerous trials and tribulations he ended up in Spain where another expat, László Kubala, had been ensconced for Galacticos team. Kubala centred on Barcelona, but Puskás became a key part of Santiago Bernabéu's first *galácticos* years at Real Madrid, claiming multiple European Cup winners' medals.

Several developments in politics, economics and technology had made a Europe-wide competition possible by the mid-1950s. There was improvement in and widespread introduction of effective floodlights at the bigger and richer clubs across Europe. This made it possible for games to be held on winter evenings. Floodlit matches became an exciting alternative for players and supporters alike. England's first international under floodlights was in November 1955 when the last part of a game versus Spain took place with the Wembley lights on. The Football League formally ratified floodlit matches at their AGM in 1958. Floodlit football offered new options and revenue streams and, according to Geoffrey Green, a different experience with a more theatrical presentation, the ball appearing to move faster and the tall pylons in four stadium corners drawing attention to the ground for miles around. Green went so far as to describe floodlights as the fairy godmother to Europe.

Air travel was crucial to clubs fulfilling pan-European fixtures during weekdays in between domestic league matches at the weekends. The increase in the European network and reliability of air travel, excluding a small number of terrible accidents as befell Manchester United in Munich, meant that almost any journey and return within Europe and the United Kingdom was achievable in the tight timeframe that was dictated. If Glasgow Rangers were drawn to play Galatasaray of Istanbul, for example, the journey and return just wasn't feasible within a midweek window on the train.

The pan-Europe element to the expansion of club football was interesting as it went against the grain of the international political situation. At the end of World War Two, Europe had been split into two specific military, political and economic groups, each led by a superpower. The USSR dominated its satellite countries such as Poland, East Germany, Czechoslovakia and Hungary through the Warsaw Pact and Comecon. The USA similarly dominated western European nations who were tied to NATO and, in a move to lock in West Germany and France to mutual peace, there was a push for economic and political integration. Drivers for this process were the Benelux agreement of 1949 between Belgium, the Netherlands and Luxembourg and then the foundation of the European Coal and Steel Community (ECSC) in 1952. The real turning point in western Europe was in 1957 when Italy, France and West Germany along with the Benelux nations signed the Treaty of Rome and formed the European Economic Community (EEC).

Integration of nation states across different aspects of society became a driving force and sport was no different. European club football transcended the two rigid political and social systems that were rapidly developing in the 1950s. When FIFA ratified the introduction of a European Cup it didn't stop at just involving clubs from western Europe, but over a short period of time the competition took in teams from both sides of the Iron Curtain. Up to the 1950s FIFA had governed world football as it passed into a presence as a sporting Esperanto, to use James Walvin's phrase, and this universality was to continue to a new level with the initiation of the three major European club competitions and the first European Nations Cup with a mini tournament held in France in 1960.

Further Voices

AFTER THE 1954 World Cup and the developments in European club competitions there were still other voices who came forward to press for change in the English game. One man driven to bring his outline for change in the September 1955 edition of *World Sports Magazine* was Sir Joseph Percival William Mallalieu. Mallalieu was, at the time, Labour MP for Huddersfield East. He appeared to have been a keen follower of the game and, in an article titled 'Beating the Soccer Crisis', he suggested a plethora of points.

Perspective is everything and Mallalieu was mostly concerned with the 'crisis' in English league football related to the fall, or as he termed it 'crash', in attendances to 34 million a season. Attendances had dropped from their peak in the immediate postwar period and would continue to fall through to the nadir of the 1980s. Why were fans staying away from football to such a degree that 'only' 34 million went through the turnstiles in 1953/54?

Mallalieu, as you might hope for a politician, had a broader perspective on these issues than other commentators who were based within the microcosm of football itself. For Mallalieu many of the explanations were social and due to the improvements in the condition of the English working classes. The general increase in average prosperity with buoyant wages and close to full employment had created an environment where there was not the drive for boys and young men to want to be a professional footballer. In a connected point he argued that the maximum wage was a restriction in attracting young players and that large numbers of professional players did not actually attain the highest possible sum anyway. He perceived that there was a consistent decline in the role of the manager and a rise in the position of the director, with directors at many clubs doing the actual managing.

Other logical reasons that Mallalieu brought forward for his perceived general crisis in football included the cost. This, at nearly 70 years removed and the current-day exorbitant Premier League prices, does seem a somewhat incredible point. One can only imagine what the response would be if Mallalieu and other commentators from the 1950s were told that one day certain Premier League matches would be on a par with the cost of going to the opera. A consistent point made later over several decades was the clash between the armchair supporter and the 'real' fan. These points became hackneyed over the 1970s and 1980s but in the mid-1950s were still relatively fresh opinions. The two aspects were seen as innately connected by Mallalieu and others – the increase in television coverage, still in its infancy in the mid-1950s, pulling live spectators away from the stadiums, or was it the push, as Mallalieu appeared to argue, that the lack of investment in stadiums over many years had led to poor facilities which needed to be improved by the FA and Football League in order to attract fans back into the habit of watching games live.

Mallalieu turned his attention to the actual game by arguing that a further reason for diminishing crowds was the standard of play, which he felt was inferior to previous times, as has been consistently argued in commentary and analysis since the codification of the game and professionalism began. English play was contrasted by Mallalieu, with continental football and particularly Hungary, as inferior. Though, as previously covered, the average supporter in Stoke and Norwich experienced very little continental football to judge the English game against.

Mallalieu, as Meisl and others did, proposed a range of developments which, he felt, could bring an improvement to the game and increase crowds, which was his main concern. It's interesting to note that Mallalieu's recommendations were different from almost everyone else, with potentially wide-reaching impact. He asked for the chancellor to remove the Entertainment Tax so that clubs would have more money for investment into stadiums and facilities. Employment contracts, perhaps unsurprisingly for a Labour MP, had a core importance for Mallalieu, who wanted to see a return to the prewar situation for managers with longer contracts to bring stability. In terms of players' contracts, radical changes were needed for the overall betterment of the game with deals of a universal nature for all players in an equal setting, the individual to be free to negotiate their contract and the scrapping of the maximum wage. Mallalieu saw the restriction of the maximum wage as affecting the performance of top players, such as Stanley Matthews, as they were distracted away from the game on extracurricular activities to earn the amounts of money they felt they were due. His argument to remove the maximum wage as a restrictive working practice seemed obvious and accurate, but to exemplify Matthews as a player to be distracted in this manner given his single-mindedness, sacrifice and total personal dedication was somewhat counterproductive.

241

Further radical changes were presented by Mallalieu in competition formats. He proposed to reorganise the professional domestic leagues by scrapping the Third Division and its north and south regionalisations, and replacing it with newly created, stronger local leagues. On a more global level he proposed a full Great Britain league, always strongly resisted by home nation football associations, and a full European league to deeply engage in direct and regular contact with the best teams, which would be an attractive option for supporters. Interestingly, although this was written right on the cusp of the creation of the European Cup, even 70 years later a full continental-based league system, though talked about endlessly, has yet to materialise.

Critcher was a further voice for change and improvement. In his essay *Football since the War*, he quoted numerous arguments that appeared from the ether – a move to being athletes who were 100 per cent fit, gymnasts, to make the ball their slave and to think intelligently before the pass. A complete reshaping of the whole outlook of English football was required. The whole concept sounds, quite frankly, exhausting. Brian Glanville was always keen to stress that though the 6-3 defeat may have acted as a catalyst, the issues related to England's diminished football status had been in existence for decades. Journalists such as Ivan Sharpe and James Catton had been writing about these deficiencies for years but had been totally ignored. Glanville argued that there was a paradox at the heart of professionalism – several of Britain's finest coaches were consistently forced abroad where various foreign countries were glad to utilise their expertise and abilities. In *Soccer Nemesis*, Glanville was scathing that many clubs' immediate response to the 6-3 game was that there was an issue with a lack of stamina and they responded to this by increasing the laps in training.

English Club Tactics

DESPITE A focus among commentators from all areas of football on the negatives of English play and the tactics at club level, it is important to remember that not all teams did play in the old-fashioned WM structure. Though critical of England at international level in January 1953 Willy Meisl, in an article entitled 'Soccer Musical Chairs', recognised that at English club level the game was a bit more sophisticated than often concluded. Indeed, Meisl listed half of the First Division clubs who had replaced 'stone walling and a hurried kick and rush method with precision passing, controlled speed and brainy positioning'.

Sunderland, West Brom, Spurs, Burnley, Wolves, Blackpool, Portsmouth, Liverpool, Manchester United, Leicester, Huddersfield and Plymouth were all identified by Meisl as having planning in their approach to the game.

Geoffrey Green also argued that the club game in England was not all one-dimensional and brought more depth to his argument than just listing clubs. In *Soccer: The World Game*, Green theorised that fundamentally football was split into a world of two deeply conflicting philosophies – these encapsulated the maximum use of the individual and the maximum use of the ball.

In more concrete terms, Green then outlined clubs who had brought a new outlook and how this had manifested itself. Arsenal and Manchester United came in for particular attention with a game based on a combination of short and long passing which created a fluid attacking approach. Other examples of different playing styles were, according to Green, a short passing game as employed by Spurs and Preston, the long, quick pass of Wolverhampton Wanderers and the bustling, eager game of Portsmouth. Blackpool's success was built on the right-sided triangle of Matthews and Taylor with Johnston behind. Green reserved special admiration for the play of Manchester United which, he concluded, was based on constant ball movement, a flexible approach, surprise and high speed.

The Revie Plan

Hungary had a direct influence on the tactics of several English clubs though many struggled in implementation due to the high skill level required for the full effect of the Magyars' 'whirl' in midfield. One of the more high-profile direct adaptations of Hungary's style of play was Manchester City's so-called Revie Plan. City manager Les McDowall was interested in tactics and the development of the game. He focussed on his players having training sessions built around ball control and improvement of skills. The style he developed at City was based on the Hungarian team seen at Wembley where there was a clear link in passing between the defence and attack through short, accurate passing, and movement off the ball.

McDonnell designated Don Revie as the withdrawn number ten who occupied a freer role and roamed across the pitch and received passes to feet in unorthodox positions. Though known as the Revie Plan, it was a combination of efforts from management and players, particularly wing-half Ken Barnes. Indeed, there appeared to have been some controversy and, perhaps, jealousy among the Manchester City players that this development was ever termed the Revie Plan. Team-mate William Leivers claimed this gave credit where it wasn't due as it was never referred to as such at the club and was clearly due to the manager and a collection of players, including Barnes and Johnny Williamson.

Revie was one of four future England managers who was deeply affected by the 6-3 game and the Hungarians, with Alf Ramsey playing and both Ron Greenwood and Bobby Robson watching and citing the match on many occasions as a powerful influence on their football outlook. Revie wrote a 20-page chapter on this tactical approach in his autobiography *Soccer's Happy Wanderer*, emphasising that the presence and role of tactics was expanding. In the era before Walter Winterbottom there was never a 20-page chapter on one specific tactical development. No doubt if the likes of Matthews or Lawton had acquired a copy of *Soccer's Happy Wanderer* they would probably have baulked in disbelief before turning over those 20 pages unread.

However, at first the Revie Plan was a disaster, but McDowall stuck to his beliefs and the team persevered. He had tested the system out on the reserves first and once satisfied he utilised it with the first-team squad. The withdrawn number ten had also been tried in a one-off situation when the Football League played the League of Ireland in an autumn 1954 fixture in Dublin. The pinnacle of the use and effectiveness of the Revie Plan came in Manchester City's 3-1 victory in the 1956 FA Cup Final against Birmingham City. Revie only actually played in the final due to the misfortune of Billy Spurdle and he positioned himself, to quote journalist H.D. Davies – aka

'The Old International' – in a deep midfield role where he could receive the ball from Bert Trautmann's direct throws and forward it to team-mates further upfield.

In an age when tactical analysis, or more accurately often semi-analysis, is at total overkill, what seems most interesting about the so-called Revie Plan is that it worked. The gap between the 6-3 match where Hidegkuti's positioning was concluded as being the major reason for Hungary's victory and the FA Cup of 1956 was two and a half years, not two and a half months, and Manchester City had been playing their specific system for a considerable period of time. That Birmingham were somewhat undone by this approach is evidence for the argument that not all teams were focussing on tactical awareness and watching new developments and that different coaches and clubs were very much at differing levels of sophistication throughout the 1950s.

Passovotchka

THE HUNGARIANS were endlessly feted in the press and among English supporters and followers in the aftermath of the 6-3 game, but it is important to remember that they were not the first team from the communist bloc of European states to impress British fans. It was just that the previous tour of a high-performing team from a communist-controlled state in the postwar period had effectively been forgotten. There had been another team who brought excitement and interest to Britain – Dynamo Moscow and their style of play termed *Passovotchka*. A main difference was that when they arrived in Britain in 1945 the standing of the USSR and the sacrifice of the Red Army during World War Two was still thought of very highly in Britain. Nazism had only recently been defeated across continental Europe and the British people knew that a major reason for this was down to the 20 million plus dead of the USSR. The passage of the eight years up to 1953 had changed things considerably in terms of the relationship between the USA and the USSR and their satellite allies. Hungary had been part of *Mitteleuropa* with the intellectual and artistic core of Vienna, Prague and Budapest, but now the ideological descriptive process had redrawn the position of Hungary from central Europe to eastern Europe, 'protected' by the USSR.

Dynamo Moscow had originally been founded by British textile workers in the 1880s, but the highly organised outfit that arrived in Britain in November 1945, though the overarching feeling was fraternal, were without question the representatives of Stalinist Russia. Were they professionals or amateurs? Were they a de facto Soviet national team? The answer was that no one in Britain really had a clue. They were different and exotic to British eyes and extremely popular as the huge crowds who attended prove. The Dynamo team brought a level of professionalism and straightforward gamesmanship not regularly seen in Britain. With their different style of play and different outlook, Dynamo showed a template for how football at the pinnacle in Europe had advanced dramatically. Instead, most observers and commentators focussed on the otherness of Dynamo – their foreignness and exoticism or their unusual level of demands which was encapsulated in their '14 Points'. This was a specific list of requirements which brought a dumbfounded response from most football followers in Britain.

The response and appreciation of Dynamo set a pattern which was interestingly replicated eight years later with the full range of reactions from seeing the Russians as innovators in the game to those who saw them as nothing special who couldn't hold a candle to British teams of the interwar period. Unsurprisingly, the internationalist Stanley Rous saw Dynamo in positive terms. In his autobiography *Football Worlds*, published 30 years after the Russians' visit, he still clearly held them in high regard.

Rous focussed on how even he was quite surprised by how different their outlook and practical approach to the game were. He assessed them as having a driving energy with a high work rate on the pitch. This was linked to an interchange of responsibilities with, as Rous interpreted, their play being momentarily ten attackers and when possession was lost turning into ten defenders, a contrast to the rigidity of positional play of English teams from that period. Pre-match preparation was also very different to Rous and other English eyes, with the team only being selected after the warm-up routine which involved each player having a ball rather than just one overall as was common practice in Britain. The fact that Rous even bothered to record this matter reinforced how unusual it was. Rous and his acolyte Walter Winterbottom were convinced, after watching Dynamo play and train, that their proficiency confirmed that England and English clubs fundamentally had a considerable amount to learn from a study of European football.

Other commentators were somewhat surprised by the overall standard of the Russian play with accurate passing and fluid movement of players regularly commented on. This was the first warning and demonstration that the former pupils had at the very least become equal to the level of the previous masters. However, though the Russians raised many questions for those who were more open during their tour and in the immediate aftermath, it was clear that things returned to their insular perspective in a fairly short period of time, with a near exclusive focus on the endless domestic timetable of league matches and FA Cup glory.

What was most apparent in this clash of cultures was in the infamous '14 Points' that the Russians presented as conditions for partaking in their four-game tour of Britain. Total bemusement was the near universal response from the British football authorities and all commentators. Firstly, that the Russians produced such a list in the first place. The respected contemporary football journalist Ivan Sharpe in *40 Years in Football* reprinted the full Dynamo list. Reading it over 70 years later, it's genuinely difficult to appreciate what all the bemusement was based on. Several of the points were about off-field activities and approximately half were concerned directly with the matches. The overall emphasis was on organisation and planning, which the Soviet structure was prevalent in. For some, including Sharpe, there was something wrong or underhand with these stipulations, as if it just wasn't the way things were done or the game was played.

Only one stood out as being obvious gamesmanship and this was point D – the claim that 'they were unable to number their players', which clearly was nonsense and to their benefit. The fluidity of their *Passovotchka* style may have confused their opponents more if they had numbers on their shirts. British players were mostly used to the fixed rigidity of the WM system where the player with number 3 or 5 or 8 on their back was always positioned in the same area of the pitch.

The irony is that for all the perceived gamesmanship of the Soviets, it could be argued that it was the British teams who pulled the most obvious piece of naughty behaviour. A further point had requested that Dynamo wanted to play against Arsenal. This was a logical request given that Arsenal had dominated English club football in the prewar 1930s. Another point also seemed to be fair as it asked, 'They wished to have an assurance that the English teams would not be changed from the names submitted to them before the match, unless they were first consulted.' Dynamo got their game against Arsenal as that was a sensible piece of business for all concerned in terms of gate money. However, at short notice Arsenal, rather mysteriously, required two guest players in their line-up. Fortunately for the north Londoners it just happened that two of England's star players – Stanley Matthews and Stanley Mortensen – were somewhere in the local vicinity, perhaps enjoying a cup of tea and a toasted tea cake in a cafe, and were dragged out at a moment's notice to pull on the Arsenal shirt. The Soviets were given short shrift when they, understandably, complained about the incredible coincidence of Arsenal's need for guest players and the gaps being filled by two famous top-class performers.

In a consistent point which later became a regular theme, commentators observed that though Dynamo were a good, not great, side, what they were doing was nothing new but was recycling the style of play of earlier British teams. The *Daily Herald* was insistent that the prewar teams would have comfortably beaten Dynamo, who were assessed overall as a good but not superb team. The differences in approach and look were apparent to all. The extended 15-to-20-minute warm-up with multiple balls going through set routines and skills, a development that caused consternation among supporters and observers, was replicated eight years later by the Hungarians at Wembley. Other areas that caused comment and some embarrassment were even down to the Dynamo kit which had a large capital letter D emblazoned on the shirt, and their habit of presenting a bouquet of flowers to their opponents, which was something that absolutely no British man since Alfred the Great had experienced. The 14 points showed an assertiveness that the British teams didn't seem to expect from the Soviet Union side. Their insistence on at least one of the matches being refereed by a Russian and having their meals at the Russian Embassy were examples of this.

Geoffrey Simpson was quite dismissive of the *Passovotchka* style. He insisted all that Dynamo were doing was returning football to a more fundamental level of pass and move which was, he said, the game that the British used to play. He was equally negative about the current British game which was a 'helter-skelter of kicking and running' where accurate passing and off-the-ball movement were forgotten. In a question repeated through the 1950s it was asked who had taught this passing game to the continentals. The British, men such as Jimmy Hogan, was the response put forward so this made it less shocking that these Russians played their choreographed football as they were just the pupils to the British masters.

One or two voices and commentators did see things in a broader sense and questioned whether it was an accurate statement to say the Russians were just following British ideas from a previous generation, and even if that was true what was the genuine relevance of that? Another journalist in the national press, Stanley Walton in the *Sunday Dispatch*, commented on the larger impact of the Russian play, in the immediate aftermath of Dynamo's 10-1 annihilation of Cardiff City. The age-old debate in football at all levels after a team has been badly beaten has always been reduced to were they so good or were we so bad? In this specific case Walton concluded it was a combination of the two. He argued that the key was coaching on the fundamental principles of the game and that this was exactly what the FA should be doing. It was a prescient point in 1945 as this was exactly what Stanley Rous was pushing for. Walton wanted to see a return to the basics being achieved to a proficient level and this could only become a reality by the roll-out of a national coaching structure to schools and clubs, which was exactly the role Winterbottom would fulfil in the near future.

In a wholly damning piece, Walton also took aim at the professionals of the game stating that they were too complacent, and that many didn't think about football and its development. He was no fan of the approach in England, with a focus on running around the pitch in an aimless manner rather than thinking about the game and its more subtle execution.

Perhaps the most important point about the Dynamo visit was its lack of genuine impact. During the tour and immediately afterwards there was huge interest from the fans and journalists, but what was the lasting legacy? The definition of complacency is that once the immediate exoticism of the Dynamo tour had died down there was no longer-lasting impact, from the euphoria of locked-out crowds and fans climbing walls and pylons to get any sort of view of the match to a quick return to the insular English game. No English team attempted to initiate the *Passovotchka* style or make wholesale changes to their training regime. Such broad concepts as Dynamo's alleged several weeks of pre-season training in the Caucasus were not implemented.

There were a few minor attempts by some clubs to introduce some of the different approaches they'd seen from the Muscovites. At the end of November 1945 Queens Park Rangers introduced the full pre-match warm-up that Dynamo had startled the British crowds with, as they came out 15 to 20 minutes before kick-off. Eight years later when the Hungarians came out at Wembley and did their pre-match routine it caused the same discombobulation among the crowd and the likes of Kenneth Wolstenholme and Tom Finney in the commentary box. They all claimed that no one had ever done anything like it before, but they were wrong. They had just all forgotten about the men from the Soviet Union in their deep blue shirts with the large D on the front from 1945.

Long-Term Aftermath
and Identity

INTERESTINGLY, IN the aftermath of the match the *FA Bulletin* used a very similar phrase to the previously mentioned Richard Weight's 'Agincourt in reverse', stating that the Hungarian defeat was the 'Spanish Armada in reverse', which connected the fixture to the glories and disasters of endless military conflict. In addition to this radical conclusion, Weight also argued in *Patriots: National Identity in Britain 1940–2000* that there were three long-term effects of football's rise in supremacy, which came from the starting point of this fixture. These were the accelerating of the waning of imperialist loyalties, a repositioning of England's engagement to the European continent, and the rise in football's popularity which replaced the institutions of parliament and monarchy as the core element of English identity. This new focus on football as a core attribute led to a more intense relationship between England and Scotland.

When Puskás, Hidegkuti *et al* were jubilantly walking off the Wembley pitch little did they know that they had altered the future trajectory of Britishness and the reduction of imperialist loyalties. The re-evaluation that the 6-3 defeat and the 7-1 loss in Budapest brought were primarily based on the football field and though the English had always looked down on the foreigner, these two huge defeats and the level of play of teams such as Uruguay in the 1954 World Cup showed that the idea that English football occupied a singular place on Mount Olympus was nothing but a delusion.

The visionary football writer David Goldblatt took a similar position to Weight. The full cultural impact of the England team was only initiated following the 6-3 defeat. Goldblatt connected this result to Britain's reduction in world power after World War Two and the slow disintegration of the global empire as nation state after nation state gained independence. The Suez Canal crisis of 1956 was the major catalyst for the *realpolitik* of the UK's position in the world. The connection that Goldblatt stressed was the unique way in which it was only England of the four home nations who had their international football results closely linked to the diminishing and destruction of the British Empire, though the British imperial structure in military and bureaucratic terms had involved individuals from all over the British Isles.

Crolley and Hand, in *Football and European Identity*, also identified the 6-3 defeat as having an important impact on imperial confidence, and said it was a core event in the development of a crisis in confidence in England's football supremacy. They interpreted the 6-3 as a singular event that transformed English football and 'precipitated a spell of self-inquiry into the antiquated tactical style of play'. The core issue for non-appreciation of other countries' football styles and development came from the origins of the game being British. The structured, organised and professional roots of football were undeniably British and were spread, as were many other sports, through imperial reach. Britain perceived itself as the sun, the never-ending mother, the creator. This cultural imperialist position led to not just a non-appreciation of other approaches to the development of football, but a total non-awareness that anything could encroach on the superiority of the mother country.

Percy Young was another prolific football writer who, in 1968, placed the 6-3 defeat in a larger post-imperial framework with the new perceived tumbling of effectiveness of the English national team representing a more general crisis in British imperialism. As Young succinctly worded it, this 'was born of a realisation that Britain does not stand where she did'. Overall, a combination of the two Hungary defeats and the 1954 World Cup acted as a point of reference that over the next 70 years linked the fortunes of the English national team to those of the nation, and Englishness for better or worse.

The connection between the Wembley defeat and the annihilation in Budapest is hardly ever mentioned, and the declinism of British imperial power has been a regular theme covered by several commentators since 1953. Matthew Taylor in *The Association Game* interpreted 1953 as a decisive moment in the relationship between English identity and football. Interestingly, it was the reduction of empire that was connected to the Hungarian victory and not the clash between capitalist and communist political systems.

The success, or not, of the English national team was perceived to have a broader nationalist context through the 1950s, in a development that found its almost ludicrous end point in the tabloid reporting of the England national team. *Daily Express* reporter Desmond Hackett and Peter Wilson from the *Daily Mirror* were among the first to introduce this specific approach. In the immediate aftermath of the 6-3 match several journalists completed a 180-degree U-turn of their positions, from England being able to brush aside the fancy dan Johnny foreigners to a position of unforgiving negativity the day after. The metaphor was established connecting the performance and result of the national team with the way England and the English should perceive themselves. As John Williams and Steven Wagg pointed out in *British Football and Social Change*, 'Fleet Street spoke as if a still great nation was being betrayed by the bunglers and shirkers who ran, or were, its football team.' A template was set which increased in its intensity and vitriol, particularly heaped on the incumbent of the England manager's position, which climaxed to the point of hysteria towards individuals such as Graham Taylor and Steve McClaren.

The image of nationalism and identity was often forged in the national media. Football had developed through media representation in print, radio and film to act as a central point for national unity. The working population were deeply engaged in this process – sometimes content, sometimes angry, but always engaged with public spectacles of skill and achievement with deep patriotic symbolism as part of the equation. Author Nicholas Fishwick agreed that football attained a central position in society which was formerly occupied by religious practice, and for some of the population football was a religion with its codes and practice and weekly pattern which set individuals in a near endless repetitious cycle only reinforced in the 1950s by the spectacular popularity of the football pools and their promises of life-changing winnings.

In contrast to the position Weight and Goldblatt placed on the Hungary defeats in developing Englishness was an article from 1954 in *The Times* which analysed the back-to-back humiliations. The writer concluded, 'If football's place in the national culture is lost, the game will lose as a sport and a game.' An unusual analysis in its stress on the business element of football being of paramount importance, but then *The Times* of 1954 was hardly the vanguard of working-class culture.

Conclusion

THE 1953/54 season was a disaster for England – regulation wins against Northern Ireland and Wales, the two awful displays and results against Hungary, two bizarre 4-4 draws with a FIFA Select XI and Belgium and a 4-2 World Cup exit to Uruguay with a colossal 30 international goals conceded in one season. Though the famous 6-3 defeat is the focus of that campaign and later, it's important to remember what happened as a whole. During the course of this particular season it became apparent to many that the discrepancies and the shortcomings could not be glossed over as the defeat to the USA in the 1950 World Cup had been.

The 6-3 and 7-1 destructions and the 1954 World Cup were important pointers in the journey where coaching, training, tactics and general preparation eventually won out. Walter Winterbottom was the effective starting point for this process with his national coaching programmes and discussion sessions, and over time he took more and more players along with him, though it took over a decade to get rid of the selection committee completely. The long, slow process of phasing out the non-coached old school, those who castigated Winterbottom, was only completed in the national team in 1957 with Stanley Matthews's last game against Denmark.

The memory of the 6-3 loss developed as a series of myths from an hour after the final whistle was blown. The overwhelming role of Hidegkuti playing the removed striker, the Puskás tummy and his drag-back goal were all central to this myth creation to the detriment of a more accurate assessment with the central position for Hungary's overwhelming success being due to their teamwork and off-the-ball movement. The core of assessment and myth creation were the voices of those who experienced the game directly, primarily the 11 English players on duty that misty north London day. The recorded thoughts and opinions of the players show us the complexity of analysing a match, even one with a seemingly comprehensive outcome. There was not a clear voice as to what happened, how the Hungarians played, who in the England team was responsible for the defeat and what was to be done about it.

The memory of the 6-3 match, as recorded through the experiences of those on the pitch, was a multiplicity of responses – from those with no voice (Eckersley), a limited voice (Robb, Sewell, Taylor), a neutral voice (Dickinson), a progressive voice (Ramsey, Wright, Mortensen), a negative voice (Matthews, Johnston) and a self-described all-encompassing voice (Merrick). The range of conclusion and memory was present in just those members of one team. Each added to the lasting memory of the 6-3 match and, not only, its relevance but more importantly interpretations, which were often of a base level of trying to pass responsibility to other players or parts of the team – from defence to attack and from attack to defence.

The position of the defeat was key in the continuum where the changers increased their leverage over the remainers. This balance had tipped from 1946 onwards with the re-membership of FIFA and the glorious team to the utter debacle of the 1950 World Cup with the unsurpassable, worst ever result in England's international history, the double Hungarian destructions of 1953/54 and the further lessons from the Switzerland World Cup. Winterbottom was the key figure who laid the groundwork for change, mostly through his position as head of coaching. This finally brought about a new approach for the team as they competed in the now truly world game. Over time players were brought into the setup for whom coaching had a daily relevance. In addition was the central impact that the 6-3 match had on those inside Wembley who later had a considerable presence on the game, primarily in England but also Scotland from the 1960s onwards – Alf Ramsey, Jimmy Hill, Jock Stein, Ron Greenwood, Bobby Robson and Malcolm Allison.

The 6-3 match was not a before-and-after experience as has so often been presented. Not all English club sides had rigidly played WM every week, and some managers and players thought about the game, but its almost unprecedented coverage and contemporary analysis, even when some conclusions were inaccurate, acted as a catalyst to the processes of change that were already happening in pockets. The increased interaction between English club sides and continental ones increased dramatically relatively soon after 1953 and with these new regular experiences came an increased flow of new ideas that meant that aspects of the 6-3 game that were commonly held as revolutionary, such as kit or pre-match warm-up, became standard.

Bibliography

Archard, L. *Hungarian Uprising. Budapest's Cataclysmic Twelve Days, 1956.* (Barnsley: Pen and Sword, 2018).

Armfield, J. *Right Back to the Beginning. The Autobiography.* (London: Headline, 2005).

Barclay, P. *Sir Matt Busby. The Definitive Biography.* (London: Ebury, 2017).

Bebber, B. (Editor) *Leisure and Cultural Conflict in Twentieth Century Britain.* (Manchester: Manchester University Press, 2012).

Bedarida, F. *A Social History of England 1851–1990.* (London: Routledge, 1991).

Benson, J. *The Rise of Consumer Society 1880–1980.* (Harlow: Longman, 1994).

Booth, G. 'Robb Gains his Spurs'. *World Sports Magazine.* October 1954.

Borsay, P. *A History of Leisure.* (Basingstoke: Palgrave, 2006).

Bourke, J. *Working Class Cultures in Britain 1890–1960. Gender, Class and Ethnicity.* (London: Routledge, 1994).

Bowler, D. *Three Lions on the Shirt. Playing for England.* (London: Orion, 2000).

Bowler, D. *Winning Isn't Everything. A Biography of Sir Alf Ramsey.* (London: Gollancz, 1998).

Bowler, D. and Reynolds, D. *Ron Reynolds. The Life of a 1950s Footballer.* (London: Orion, 2003).

Brailsford, D. *British Sport: A Social History*. (Cambridge: Lutterworth Press, 1992).

Briggs, S. *Don't Mention the Score. A Masochist's History of the England Football Team*. (London: Quercus, 2008).

Buchan, C. *A Lifetime in Football*. (Edinburgh: Mainstream, 2010).

Buchan, C. *Charles Buchan's Soccer Gift Book 1953-54*. (London: Charles Buchan Publishing, 1953).

Buchan, C. *Charles Buchan's Soccer Gift Book 1954-55*. (London: Charles Buchan Publishing, 1954).

Bukovi and Csaknardy. *Learn to Play the Hungarian Way*. (Budapest: Hungarian Sport Publishing House, 1954).

Burk, K. *The British Isles since 1945*. (Oxford: Oxford University Press, 2003).

Butler, B. *The Official History of the Football Association*. (London: Queen Anne Press, 1991).

Calley, R. *Blackpool. The Complete Record*. (Derby: Derby Books, 2011).

Carter, N. *The Football Manager. A History*. (London: Routledge, 2006).

Cartledge, B. *The Will to Survive. A History of Hungary*. (London: Timewell Press, 2006).

Charlton, B. *My England Years. The Autobiography*. (London: Headline, 2008).

Clarke, P. *Hope and Glory. Britain 1900–2000*. (London: Penguin, 2004).

Collins, T. *Sport in Capitalist Society. A Short History*. (Abingdon: Routledge, 2013).

Connolly, K. & MacWilliam, R. *Fields of Glory, Paths of Gold. The History of European Football*. (Edinburgh: Mainstream, 2005).

Cooper, M. *Pompey People. Portsmouth FC Who's Who 1899–2000*. (Harefield: Yore Publishing, 2000).

Cresswell, P. & Evans. S. *European Football: A Fan's Handbook*. (London: Penguin, 1997).

Crolley, L. & Hand, D. *Football and European Identity. Historical Narratives Through the Press*. (Abingdon: Routledge, 2006).

Crouch, T. *The World Cup. The Complete History*. (London: Aurum, 2006).

Csanadi, A. *Soccer*. (Budapest: Athenaeum, 1965).

Daniels, R. *Blackpool. The Official Club History*. (London: Robert Hale, 1972).

Dasgupta, S. *Salaam. Stanley Matthews*. (London: Granta, 2006).

Delaney, T. *A Century of Soccer*. (London: Heinemann, 1963).

Downing, D. *Passovotchka: Moscow Dynamo in Britain 1945*. (London: Bloomsbury, 1999).

Edworthy, N. *The Second Most Important Job in the Country*. (London: Virgin, 1999).

FA Book for Boys 1953-54. (London: Naldrett Press, 1953).

FA Book for Boys 1954-55. (London: Naldrett Press, 1954).

Farror, M. & Lamming, D. *A Century of English International Football 1872–1972*. (London: Robert Hale, 1972).

Ferrier, B. *Soccer Partnership. Billy Wright and Walter Winterbottom.* (London: Sportsman's Book Club, 1961).

Fishwick, N. *English Football and Society 1910–1950*. (Manchester: Manchester University Press, 1989).

Finney, T. *My Autobiography*. (London: Headline, 2003).

Forrest, A.J. 'The Hungarian Triumph'. *FA Bulletin*. December 1953. pp.20-24.

Galeano, E. *Football in Sun and Shadow*. (London: Penguin, 2018).

Gibbs, N. *England. The Football Facts*. (Exeter: Facer, 1988).

Giller, N. *Billy Wright. A Hero for All Seasons.* (London: Robson Books, 2002).

Giller, N. *Footballing Fifties.* (London: JR Books, 2007).

Giulianotti, R. *Football a Sociology of the Global Game.* (Cambridge: Polity Press, 1999).

Glanville, B. *Champions of Europe. The History, Romance and Intrigue of the European Cup.* (Enfield: Guinness, 1991).

Glanville, B. *England Managers. The Toughest Job in Football.* (London: Headline, 2007).

Glanville, B. 'Football at Wembley' in *The Official Wembley Story of Fifty Years.* (London: Sportsworld, 1973).

Glanville, B. *Football Memories. Over 50 Years of the Beautiful Game.* (London: Robson, 2004).

Glanville, B. 'It's Brains We Want. The Problem of British Soccer.' *World Sports Magazine.* December 1954. p.17.

Glanville, B. 'Revolution in Coventry.' *World Sports Magazine.* November 1955. pp.22-23.

Glanville, B. *Soccer Nemesis.* (London: Secker and Warberg, 1955).

Glanville, B. (Editor) *The Footballer's Companion.* (London: Eyre and Spottiswode, 1962).

Glanville, B. *The Story of the World Cup.* (London: Faber and Faber, 1993).

Goldblatt, D. *The Ball is Round. A Global History of Football.* (London: Viking, 2006).

Goldblatt, D. *The Game of Our Lives. The Meaning and Making of English Football.* (London: Penguin, 2015).

Golesworthy, M. *The Encyclopaedia of Association Football.* (London: Robert Hale, 1967).

Goodwin, B. *The Spurs Alphabet. A Complete Who's Who of Tottenham Hotspur.* (Leicester: Polar Publishing, 1992).

Green, G. *Soccer in the Fifties.* (Shepperton: Ian Allen, 1974).

Green, G. *Soccer. The World Game.* (London: Sportsman's Book Club, 1954).

Griffith, E. 'Gilbert Merrick. The Born Goalkeeper.' *World Sports Magazine.* March 1954. pp.26-27.

Hall, S. *1956.* (London: Faber and Faber, 2016).

Hargraves, J. *Sport, Power and Culture. A Social and Historical Analysis of Popular Sports in Britain.* (Cambridge: Polity Press, 1986).

Hayes, D. *England. The Football Facts. Players, Teams, Matches, Goals, Results. The Ultimate England Reference Book.* (London: Michael O'Mara Books, 2008).

Henderson, J. *The Wizard. The Life of Stanley Matthews.* (London: Random House, 2013).

Henderson, J. *When Footballers Were Skint. A Journey in Search of the Soul of Football.* (London: Biteback, 2018).

Hobsbawm, E. & Ranger, T. (Editors) *The Invention of Tradition.* (Cambridge: Cambridge University Press, 1994).

Holt, R. *Sport and the British. A Modern History.* (Oxford: Clarendon, 1992).

Holt, R. & Mason, T. *Sport in Britain 1945–2000.* (Oxford: Blackwell, 2000).

Hopcraft, A. *The Football Man.* (London: Simon and Schuster, 1988).

Jeffs, P. *Pompey's Gentleman Jim.* (Derby: Breedon, 1998).

Jeffs, P. *The Golden Age of Football.* (Derby: Breedon, 1991).

Johnston, H. *The Rocky Road to Wembley.* (London: Sportsman's Book Club, 1954).

Keeton, G.W. *The Football Revolution. A Study of the Changing Pattern of Association Football.* (Newton Abbot: David and Charles, 1972).

Kelly, S.F. *A Game of Two Halves.* (London: Mandarin, 1993).

Kitto, H.D.F. *The Greeks.* (London: Penguin, 1962).

Kynaston, D. *Family Britain 1951–57*. (London: Bloomsbury, 2009).

Kynaston, D. *Modernity Britain. Book 1. 1957–59.* (London: Bloomsbury, 2013).

Kynaston, D. *Modernity Britain. Book 2 1959–62.* (London: Bloomsbury, 2014).

Lloyd, G. *One Cap Wonders. The Ultimate Claim to Football Fame.* (London: Robson Books, 2001).

Lofthouse, N. *Goals Galore.* (London: Stanley Paul, 1954).

Macpherson, A. *Jock Stein. The Definitive Biography.* (Newbury: Highdown, 2004).

McKinstry, L. *Sir Alf. A Major Reappraisal of the Life and Times of England's Greatest Football Manager.* (London: Harper Collins, 2006).

Malam, C. *Clown Prince of Soccer? The Len Shackleton Story.* (Newbury: Highdown, 2004).

Mallalieu, J.P.W. 'Beating the Soccer Crisis.' *World Sports Magazine.* September 1955. pp.32-33.

Marr, A. *A History of Modern Britain.* (London: Macmillan, 2007).

Marwick, A. *British Society Since 1945.* (London: Penguin, 1945).

Mason, T. 'A Particularly Depressing Day: 29 June 1950, USA 1 England 0.' *Soccer History.* Issue 25.

Mason, T. *Sport in Britain.* (London: Faber and Faber, 1988).

Matthews, S. *Back in Touch. An Autobiography.* (London: Arthur Baker, 1980).

Matthews, S. *Feet First.* (London: Ewan and Dale, 1948).

Matthews, S. *Feet First Again.* (London: Kaye and Company, 1952).

Matthews, S. *The Stanley Matthews Story.* (London: Oldbourne, 1960).

Matthews, S. *The Way It Was.* (London: Headline, 2000).

Meisl, W. 'Don't Shelf These Resolutions.' *World Sports Magazine*. October 1954. pp.17-18.

Meisl, W. 'Fateful Goals.' *World Sports Magazine*. February 1953.

Meisl, W. 'Fight or Football?' *World Sports Magazine*. January 1955. pp.7-9.

Meisl, W. 'Match of the (Three Quarter) Century.' *World Sports Magazine*. August 1955. pp.36-37.

Meisl, W. 'Olympic Champions at Wembley.' *World Sports Magazine*. November 1953.

Meisl, W. 'Soccer Musical Chairs.' *World Sports Magazine*. January 1953.

Meisl, W. *Soccer Revolution*. (London: Phoenix Sports Books, 1955).

Meisl, W. 'Stanley Matthews. Gentleman and Genius.' *World Sports Magazine*. April 1954. p.5.

Meisl, W. 'The Battle for Soccer Supremacy.' *World Sports Magazine*. June 1954. pp.16-17.

Meisl, W. 'The Road to Recovery.' *World Sports Magazine*. January 1954. pp.5-7.

Meisl, W. 'The Welcome Invaders.' *World Sports Magazine*. January 1955. pp.15-17.

Merrick, G. *I See it All*. (London: Museum Press, 1954).

Miller, D. *England's Last Glory. The Boys of '66*. (London: Pavilion, 2006).

Montgomery, J. *The Fifties*. (London: Allen and Unwin, 1965).

Morse, G. *Sir Walter Winterbottom. The Father of Modern English Football*. (London: John Blake Publishing, 2016).

Mortensen, S. *Football is My Game*. (London: Sampson, 1949).

Mourant, A. *Don Revie: Portrait of a Footballing Enigma*. (London: Mainstream, 2003).

Moynihan, J. *The Soccer Syndrome*. (London: Sportsman's Book Club, 1968).

Murray, B. *The World's Game. A History of Soccer*. (Illinois: University of Illinois Press, 1998).

Oliver, G. *The Guinness Book of World Soccer*. (London: Guinness Publishing, 1995).

Official FA Yearbook. 1953-54. (London, Naldrett Press, 1953).

Official FA Yearbook. 1954-55. (London: Naldrett Press, 1954).

Pawson, T. *The Goalscorers*. (London: Cassell, 1978).

Payne, M. *England. The Complete Post War Record*. (Derby: Breedon, 1993).

Penney, I. *England's Football Legends*. (Derby: Breedon, 2004).

Polley, M. *Moving the Goalposts. A History of Sport and Society Since 1945*. (London: Routledge, 1998).

Pringle, P. (Editor). *The Boys' Book of Soccer for 1953*. (London: Evans Brothers, 1952).

Pringle, P. (Editor). *The Boys' Book of Soccer for 1954*. (London: Evans Brothers, 1953).

Pringle, P. (Editor). *The Boys' Book of Soccer for 1955*. (London: Evans Brothers, 1954).

Pugh, M. *State and Society. A Social and Political History of Britain since 1870*. (London: Hodder, 2008).

Puskas, F. 'I Tip England.' *World Sports Magazine*. November 1954. pp.5-7.

Ramsey, A. *Talking Football*. (London: Stanley Paul, 1952).

Rippon, A. *Eng-land! The Story of the National Soccer Team*. (Ashbourne: Moorland, 1981).

Robbins, K. *The British Isles. 1901–51*. (Oxford: Oxford University Press, 2002).

Robson, B. *Against the Odds. An Autobiography*. (London: Stanley Paul, 1991).

Rogan, J. *The Football Managers*. (London: Queen Anne Press, 1989).

Rous, S. *Football Worlds. A Lifetime in Sport*. (London: Faber and Faber, 1978).

Russell, D. *Football and the English*. (Preston: Carnegie, 1997).

Scovell, B. *The England Managers. The Impossible Job*. (Stroud: Tempus, 2006).

Sharpe, I. *Forty Years in Football*. (London: Sportsman's Book Club, 1954).

Shindler, C. *Four Lions. The Lives and Times of Four Captains of England*. (London: Head of Zeus, 2017).

Smith, R. *Mister: The Men Who Taught the World how to Beat England at Their Own Game*. (London: Simon and Schuster, 2006).

Soccer Monthly Annual 1980. (London: IPC Magazines, 1979).

Stratton, S. & Hecht, E. *International Football Book Number 5*. (London: Souvenir Press, 1963).

Szollosi, G. *Puskas*. (Glasgow: Freight Books, 2015).

Taylor, M. *The Association Game. A History of British Football*. (Harlow: Pearson Education, 2008).

Taylor, M. *The Leaguers. The Making of Professional Football in England 1900–1939*. (Liverpool: Liverpool University Press, 2005).

Taylor, R. & Ward, A. *Kicking and Screaming. An Oral History of Football in England*. (London: Robson Books, 1995).

Tennant, J. *Football: The Golden Age. Extraordinary Images from 1900 to 1985*. (London: Cassell, 2001).

Todd, S. *The People. The Rise and Fall of the Working Class*. (London: John Murray, 2015).

Tomlinson, A. *The Game's Up. Essays in the Cultural Analysis of Sport, Leisure and Popular Culture*. (Aldershot: Ashgate, 1999).

Tossell, D. *The Great English Final. 1953: Cup, Coronation and Stanley Matthews.* (Durrington: Pitch, 2013).

Traverso, E. *Fire and Blood. The European Civil War 1914–45.* (London: Verso, 2017).

Wade, A. *The FA Guide to Training and Coaching.* (London: Heinemann, 1981).

Wagg, S. *The Football World. A Contemporary Social History.* (Brighton: Harvester, 1984).

Walvin, J. *Football and the Decline of Britain.* (Basingstoke: Macmillan, 1986).

Walvin, J. *Leisure and Society.* (London: Longman, 1978).

Walvin, J. *The People's Game.* (Edinburgh: Mainstream, 1994).

Ward, A. & Williams, J. *Football Nations. Sixty Years of the Beautiful Game.* (London: Bloomsbury, 2010).

Ward, P. *Britishness Since 1870.* (Abingdon: Routledge, 2004).

Watt, T. & Palmer, K. *Wembley the Greatest Stage. The Official History of 75 Years at Wembley Stadium.* (London: Simon and Schuster, 1998).

Weight, R. *Patriots. National Identity in Britain 1940–2000.* (London: Macmillan, 2002).

Williams, J. & Wagg, S. (Editors) *British Football and Social Change. Getting into Europe.* (Leicester: Leicester University Press, 1991).

Williams, R. *The Perfect 10. Football's Dreamers, Schemers, Playmakers and Playboys.* (London: Faber and Faber, 2006).

Wilson, A.N. *The Age of Elizabeth II.* (London: Hutchinson, 2008).

Wilson, B. *You've Got to be Crazy.* (London: Weidenfeld and Nicolson, 1989).

Wilson, J. *Behind the Curtain. Travels in Eastern European Football.* (London: Orion, 2006).

Wilson, J. *Inverting the Pyramid. The History of Football Tactics*. (London: Orion, 2008).

Wilson, J. *The Anatomy of England. A History in Ten Matches*. (London: Orion, 2010).

Winner, D. *Those Feet. An Intimate History of English Football*. (London: Bloomsbury, 2005).

Winterbottom, W. *Soccer Coaching. An Official Publication of the FA*. (London: Heinemann, 1962).

Wright, B. *Captain of England*. (London: Stanley Paul, 1950).

Wright, B. *Football is My Passport*. (London: Stanley Paul, 1957).

Wright, B. *One Hundred Caps and All That*. (London: Robert Hale, 1962).

Wright, B. *The World's My Football Pitch*. (London: Stanley Paul, 1953).

Young, P.M. *A History of British Football*. (London: Sportsman's Books, 1968).